PRIESTHOOD
PRAYER
Learning to Pray Like Christ

PRIESTHOOD
PRAYER
Learning to Pray Like Christ

ADIA TALIAFERRO

MYND
MATTERS

Books may be purchased in quantity and/or special sales by contacting the author.

Mynd Matters Publishing
715 Peachtree Street NE, Suites 100 & 200, Atlanta, GA 30308
www.myndmatterspublishing.com

ISBN-13: 978-1-948145-22-0 (pbk)
e-ISBN: 978-1-948145-23-7

FIRST EDITION

I dedicate this book to the women in my life who have mentored me spiritually and set an example of what it means to be an intercessor. They have encouraged me over the years to grow in my gift of prayer and intercession: my mother, Bettye Taliaferro, Susan T. James, Kenlyn Brown, Ernie Batchelor and April Ingram.

Contents

Introduction

Do you ever feel like throwing in the towel on your prayer life? Have you ever been annoyed with yourself because you failed to pray the way you may have promised yourself and God you would? No matter how good your intentions are to spend more time in prayer, you fail to do it because it seems like nothing is happening...or you fall asleep.

Maybe you don't pray because you just don't believe prayer works. You've experienced major disappointments when you've prayed for people or things, and it seems like your prayers have gone unanswered. Maybe, for you, it's not about discouragement or a dry prayer life. Maybe you think, "How do I begin to develop a real connection with God? How do I begin to talk to Him and what should I talk about?" You may feel like God just doesn't get it—He doesn't understand what you feel. You may have been taught that Jesus understands everything you go through, but you don't feel like He understands your struggle since He lived a perfect human life. So why develop a deeper connection with a deity that doesn't completely *get* you?

Know this: you're not alone in your struggles. Most people who have or desire a rich prayer life have experienced at least one of the above. I have. It's the reason I wrote this book. It has been birthed from experiencing all of the aforementioned feelings and many more.

One day as I was praying, I expressed to God that I felt my prayers were dry and apologized for falling asleep on Him. I asked Him to help me overcome falling asleep during prayer as He had helped the disciples. You may recall how the disciples fell asleep on the Mount of Transfiguration when they should have been praying with Christ. You may also remember when Jesus asked them to pray with Him in Gethsemane before His crucifixion, they fell asleep. But later on, in the book of Acts, we can see that they have grown and become fervent in their prayer life in the upper room before Pentecost occurs. Another time they are seen going to the temple to pray at three o'clock in the afternoon! [1]

In addition to asking God to help me to stop falling asleep, I had a second request about my prayer life. I asked Him to help me experience prayer as Christ experienced prayer. As I prayed, the Holy Spirit prompted me to write a book about it. I decided to use my morning devotional time to meditate on scripture, study, and let God lead me in sharing what He was teaching me. He led me to study about Jesus as our High Priest in the book of Hebrews. Studying helped me see different aspects of Christ's experience as both man and God, aspects I had never realized. Writing *Priesthood Prayer* has helped me grow more in love with Christ and develop a deeper appreciation for everything He experienced on behalf of humanity. I know now that Christ does understand the human experience. After going through this intense study of Christ's experience in prayer, there is no question or doubt that can tempt me to think otherwise. Instead of simply having "head knowledge," my heart now truly grasps it. When I pray now and thank Him for His sacrifice, it's not perfunctory. There is a depth of gratitude. Understanding how much the Savior needed to pray showed me how much more we, as Christ-followers, need to pray. Writing this devotional renewed my desire and commitment to continually intercede for others.

---

[1] Lk. 9:26-28; Mt. 26:26-46; Ac. 1:12-14; Ac. 2:1; Ac. 3:1

This 21-day devotional focuses on:

- how Christ wrestled and surrendered to remain sinless through constant, prayerful connection with the Father, by the power of the Holy Spirit
- the victory we have in Him because of the victory He gained for us over sin
- how He intercedes for us as the High Priest
- how we are to follow His example and intercede for others
- the reason Jesus chose to identify with us—because of God's unfailing, unconditional love for humanity to save us

There are four different sections to this devotional. The first is about communion with God. The second is about how Christ identified with humanity. The third explains the priesthood of intercession. The fourth explains our victory in Christ.

Each devotional thought consists of: a Bible text, a devotional reading, reflection questions to reinforce the reading, and some include a prayer and exercises for spiritual growth. Many times, the meaning of a text is lost in translation. To help bring clarity and a more in-depth understanding to the selected passages of study for each day, I have provided explanations for certain words in the original language for most of the Bible verses used for each day. This will help to reveal "the life" of the words given in the selected passages. You can expect:

- practical application to grow in your relationship with God
- a renewed understanding of what it means for God's children to be intercessors

- your prayer life to be renewed for those who need "fresh wind"

- for those who have only begun to pray—a new, blossoming relationship.

I hope and pray this book will help you connect to Christ in a new way. Let's pray!

Tag's Story

I would be remiss if I did not include a word on how much our Father desires fellowship with His children. God wants an intimate relationship with all of us. No one has a monopoly on His presence. We receive His strength and are transformed into the image of His Son in His presence. He will use any means to have His children spend time with Him. He will use difficult circumstances, broken relationships, financial needs, sickness, or even an animal! That's right, an animal. He used my beloved cat, the late Taggert Thaddeus Theophilus Taliaferro, known affectionately as Tag, Taggy, and Taggy Waggy.

One day in September 2010, I was very sick. My head was pounding and my body felt weak from a persistent, dry cough. I was hoarse, dehydrated, and my eyes hurt. I needed sleep. Usually, Tag would sleep with me and wake up in the middle of the night to go to the bathroom. This means he would wake me up to let him out of my bedroom. As a loving animal parent, I would wake up and open my door to let him out. This particular night, however, it wasn't happening. I kindly told him, "Taggy, you cannot sleep with me tonight. I'm not going to get up to let you out. I need rest." I put him in the hallway and closed and locked the door behind me.

During this season in my life, God would wake me up at 3:37 a.m. to pray. That night, I told God if He wanted me to wake up to pray, He would need a miracle because I wasn't getting up on my own. After saying that, my head hit the pillow and was sound asleep.

The next thing I remember is a light tap on my elbow. I awoke to find Tag sitting on my stomach with his paw gently resting on my left elbow as my arm lay folded across my chest.

I looked at him and said, "Taggy, what are you doing in here? I thought I put you out." I then heard a still, small voice whisper, "Look at your phone." It was 3:37 a.m. As the saying goes, you could have stuck a fork in me because I was done. Mainly because:

- ➤ I had put him out and locked the door
- ➤ My cat evidently heeded a command from the Lord like Balaam's donkey[2]
- ➤ I didn't even feel him climb on top of me, just the light tap of his paw
- ➤ It was 3:37 a.m., on the dot, and God loves me so much that He unlocked my door (most likely by an angel's hand) so my cat could wake me up

I was flabbergasted to say the least. I sat up on my elbows and asked, "Taggy, were you being obedient to the Lord?" He jumped to the floor, went back out into the hallway, laid down, and went to sleep. There is no doubt in my mind that the animals got on the ark two by two![3] There is no way he unlocked the door and let himself in.

The God of the universe loves us so much and cherishes time with us that He will do what is necessary to spend time with us. He could have woken me up and not let me fall back asleep, but he didn't. He is intentional. He used my cat to show me a miracle. Just as God was intentional with me, He will do the same for you.

---

[2] Nm. 22:21-39
[3] Gn. 7:2-3,15

PART ONE

Communion and Confession:
Approaching God in Prayer

DAY
ONE

Open Communication with Our Heavenly Father

"Since we have a great high priest who has passed through the heavens, Jesus the Son of God, let us hold fast our confession. For we do not have a high priest who is unable to sympathize with our weaknesses, but one who in every respect has been tempted as we are, yet without sin. Let us then with confidence draw near to the throne of grace, that we may receive mercy and find grace to help in time of need."

—Hebrews 4:14-16 (ESV)

To pray like Christ prayed, we need to come to the Father in prayer the way He did. The first, and most important thing is to be open and honest with the Father. Many people pray while not being completely honest with God, because they are not completely honest with themselves. Some people may not know how to be honest with themselves about their feelings—whether about God, another human, or themselves. In various circumstances, most people have trouble being honest with themselves, so they're definitely not going to realize that they are not being honest with God.

Many sincere-hearted and well-intentioned Christians pray how they think God wants them to. Many may fail to ask, "Lord, teach me how to come to You in prayer so our communication can be what it needs to be. Help me the way I need to be helped."

Some Christians pray from a place of legalism because they have a faulty understanding of how to identify with Christ's resistance to temptation; they know and understand that He was tempted but not the effect it had on Him. This can lead to a pattern of prayer based on how they think He prayed instead of how He actually prayed. Often times, Christians suppress their feelings in effort to numb the tug of temptation as if the sin they are dealing with is not appealing to them. They may try to muscle up emotion to make themselves feel empowered. But that's not what Christ did. He surrendered.

Religion, unfortunately, has cast a shadow on prayer, making it seem like a burden or chore. That is not what prayer is meant to be. The heaviness of prayer is the mental and emotional anguish we can bring to it, not prayer itself. This may make us run from prayer which means we're running from God.

Hebrews 4:14-16 tells us Christ was tempted like we are tempted today. He felt everything in His flesh that we feel in ours. *Everything* we wrestle with in our flesh, He felt in His. The sins we try to overcome, He was tempted with too; even prayerlessness.

If the enemy had interfered with the Savior's connection in prayer, he could have sabotaged Christ and caused Him to abort His mission. Christ discerned the temptation projected onto Him for the lie it was. Although He was tempted to succumb, He took them to the Father and was honest about what He was feeling. Through Christ's openness, the Father was able to strengthen, refresh, encourage, and keep Him. Christ was able to give over His feelings of temptation without guilt or shame because He knew He could confidently go to him.

Christ did this for us so that we could do it. We are able to come with boldness to the throne and find grace and mercy. He surrendered for us while He lived in the flesh, receiving power and authority to extend us the help that was extended to Him. Despite the temptations, He received grace and mercy to overcome them and now we receive the same.

The definition of *boldness* in Hebrews 4:16 is "freedom of speech, openness and confidence that leaves a witness that something deserves to be remembered and taken seriously."[4] Our Father wants us to be free in our communication with Him. For Christians, freedom doesn't invite irreverence. That is, freedom does not allow for a person to approach God without respect for who He is. This freedom gives us the opportunity to communicate openly about how we feel and to ask God how He feels about the matters of the heart. Don't assume you know how God feels. His response may surprise you when you open up. Know that He gives serious consideration to your feelings.

Grace is defined in this text as "God leaning himself toward his children, ready to give himself to help them; extending himself." Mercy means "He is ready to help by his covenant loyalty."[5] God is waiting to give Himself to us the way He gave Himself to His Son. He is waiting to talk to us the way He talked to His Son. He is waiting for us to allow Him to love us the way He loved His Son.

---

[4] James Strong, "Strong's Concordance",
https://biblehub.com/greek/3954.htm, (1905)
[5] Gleason Archer and Gary Hill, Helps Word-studies,
https://biblehub.com/greek/5485.htm, (2011)

Reflection Questions

Based on today's reading:

- ➢ List some reasons people may find it intimidating to pray.
- ➢ How did Jesus approach the Father?
- ➢ What has been made available to us through Jesus?
- ➢ What is God waiting for from us?

_____

_____

_____

_____

_____

_____

_____

_____

_____

_____

_____

_____

_____

_____

_____

_____

_____

Personal Prayer

Dear Heavenly Father, I ask that you teach me to come to you as Jesus Christ did. I thank you He has done all the work for me I cannot do for myself. Please teach me how to express myself the way He did so you and I can have the same kind of relationship He had with you while He was here on Earth. Help me put away all assumptions when I come to you. Let your Holy Spirit show me how our relationship needs to change, what areas I need to be more open with you in, and how to completely trust you. Thank you for making yourself available to me. In Jesus' name, Amen.

DAY
TWO

Hold Fast to Your Confession

"Since then we have a great high priest who has passed through the heavens, Jesus, the Son of God, let us hold fast our confession."

—Hebrews 4:14 (ESV)

Hold fast to your agreement! Have you come into agreement with what God has specifically spoken over you? Do you know what God has spoken over you? Have you come into agreement with what He has spoken in His word? Christ knew who He was and what His Father had said of Him from the time He was young. He was able to hold onto what the Father said because of what He knew. When He prayed, Jesus confessed what the Father had said to Him. He repeated the truth His Father pronounced over His life in prayer to keep Himself in alignment. Jesus confessed anything that had the potential to throw Him off; anything counter to what His Father revealed to Him.

In Hebrews 4:14, *confess* is a compound word with likewise, a compound meaning in the Greek language. The word for *confess* is *homologia* which means "an agreement or confession."[6] Breaking the word into units gives a better explanation of what happens during confession. The first part *homo*, from *homou*, means "the same and together."[7] This leads us to the question when we pray, what needs to be the same and what needs to be together? We know the answers by what was mentioned of Christ in the text. Our thoughts need to be the same as God's

---

[6] Gleason Archer and Gary Hill, Helps Word- Studies, https://biblehub.com/greek/3671.htm, (2011)
[7] ibid

so we can speak what He speaks. The togetherness kicks in when we decide to come into agreement with what He is saying. God brings us to Him so that we can be on one accord with Him.

Next, *logia* comes from the word *lego* which means "to lay down to sleep." The word *lego* later took on the meaning of "laying an argument to rest, bringing a message to closure, bringing it to a conclusion."[8] It's interesting that God uses the words sleep and rest to describe the state of death for those dead in Him. When *homo* and *logia* come together, they mean our confession to God allows Him to put the things that are in us and don't align with Him to death. The proper meaning of *homologia* is "A conclusion embraced by common profession or affirmation." Our confession opens the way for death of the temptations, thoughts and lies of the enemy; the things that cause the death of the spiritual man. It is this death of the flesh that Jesus surrendered for us. As the argument comes to rest, the flesh is put to death by us saying what God has already said. Confession is putting to death what God has not said and receiving what He has said by agreeing with Him.

When Jesus prayed, He allowed whatever He wrestled with to be put to death so it would not come between Him and the Father. He presented what He was feeling. He received God's encouragement and pronouncement and laid the fight within Him to rest. Jesus always took the Father's final say; it's what He really wanted anyway. Remember, while in Gethsemane, Jesus asked God three times to take the cup from Him. God did not. In exchange for His confession, He was given the strength to go through with what God had planned so that we may have salvation.

---

[8] ibid

God tells us in Isaiah 1:18, *"Come let us reason together."* Understand that the reasoning is not for you to prove God wrong or get your way by changing His mind. It is for Him to show you His loving and all-good intentions. God uses the situations you surrender to Him to show you why His way is best and why it's important for you to believe in and agree with Him. He does this because He is working out His best in and for you.

You may not agree with God on a determined perspective—yours or His—His way of trying to work things out, His way of leading you, or the wisdom He is trying to give you. Whatever it may be, please come into agreement with Him. A lack of agreement may not be related to sin, but it would be sinful to continue to shun and doubt what He wants you to confess in agreement. Allowing the disagreement to continue will only block your blessings. When you come into agreement with what God has spoken, do not let go of it by changing your mind. Hold fast to what Hebrews 4:14 tells us.

Take some time to get into the presence of God and ask Him to show you where you need to come into agreement with Him.

If you know but have doubted and wavered, ask Him to make you firm in your agreement.

If you know but have rejected it, repent and trust.

If you don't know, let Him reveal it and receive it with gratitude.

In all of these, hold fast.

Reflection Questions

> ➢ What did Christ do to keep Himself grounded in His identity?
> ➢ What new insight did you gain from the word *homologia* that will help you grow in prayer?

Personal Growth Questions

- How will understanding Christ's practice of *homologia* help your personal relationship with the Father?
- What do you need to come into agreement with the Father on over your life today?
- Write a heartfelt prayer based on what you learned today.

_____

_____

_____

_____

_____

_____

_____

_____

_____

_____

_____

_____

_____

_____

_____

_____

PART TWO

Christ Identifying with Us:
His Nature and Struggle

DAY
THREE

His Image and Victory

"In the days of his flesh, Jesus offered up prayers and supplications, with loud cries and tears, to him who was able to save him from death, and he was heard because of his reverence."

—Hebrews 5:7 (ESV)

"Likewise the Spirit helps us in our weakness. For we do not know what to pray for as we ought, but the Spirit himself intercedes for us with groanings too deep for words. And he who searches hearts knows what is the mind of the Spirit, because the Spirit intercedes for the saints according to the will of God...Christ Jesus is the one who died—more than that, who was raised—who is at the right hand of God, who indeed is interceding for us."

— Romans 8:26-27, 34a (ESV)

After overcoming sin for us, Christ is still praying. While overcoming His flesh, His prayers were laced with complete surrender so that He could reign as Conqueror. He cried out for deliverance so He would not give into the temptations that bombarded Him. Because He persevered in His walk, He now prays victoriously. His prayers are no longer for deliverance from the temptations of Satan, but of praise, gratitude and authoritative intercession to the Father.[9] He continues to give praise and gratitude for the connection He formed with the Father that allowed Him to conquer.[10] His prayers kept Him from falling as our first parents did [Adam and Eve], and now He intercedes for us continually. Because

---

[9] Jd. 24-25
[10] Jn. 17

He overcame, we can overcome. He pleads to the Father on our behalf to keep us as the Father kept Him. The same power that kept Christ is the same power the Father wants to give us—the power of the Holy Spirit.

Through His consistency and victory, He gained the right to pray for us as High Priest when He returned to heaven. Just as the earthly high priests had to enter the Most Holy Place without sin lest they die, Jesus would have caused all of eternity to be lost if He stumbled in any way. God Himself would have had to die by His own law because He would have failed. Heaven would have been bankrupt of all its riches; all of the universe would have been undone. God would have ceased to be God. Satan would have proven God could not live by His own law; the same law Satan argued was impossible to keep. God magnifies His law and His name as one, meaning that He Himself is bound by His own standard.[11] God will not act contrary to His law for convenience the way humans do when we have high-ranking titles and authority. That would be an abuse of power. The law defines His name and the character of who He is. God lives by His own law and chooses not to live by the law of sin. If He chose to act differently, He would cease to be God. Jesus passing the test in the wilderness was important for this reason.

Since Satan could not be God, he tried to tempt Jesus to be like him so that he could then become God. Satan tried to get Jesus to conform to his image. Man was made in God's image and worshipped the Creator just as Satan did when he was Lucifer. In the testing of Jesus, Satan tried to recreate God in his image by trying to make Jesus sin.[12] He was jealous of the Savior and wanted to be Him. Since he could not be God, he

---

[11] Ps. 138:2
[12] Mt. 4:1-11, Lk. 4:1-13, Mk. 1:12-13,

tried to make God like Him. Adam and Eve, being made in the image of God, made Satan jealous because they were like God. Satan enticed them to sin, thereby counterfeiting one of the powers he was most jealous of—the power to create.

Man was made in God's image and made to procreate as God creates. Satan does not have that capacity to create. He deceived humanity so it would take on his fallen nature and bare his image. Satan, who was once the highest-commanding being in heaven, recreates our first parents with deception, hoping they would be doomed to live in their fallen state. Christ, however, came to Earth and put on the confining flesh Adam and Eve had. When Lucifer saw this, he thought it was his chance to enslave the Savior in His flesh. Satan believed if Jesus gave in to temptation, He would be remade as his offspring and bear his image and character eternally. Yet, Jesus overcame the temptations of Satan so He could transform humankind back to our original state before sin entered the world.

Satan claimed the human race as his own when Adam and Eve sinned. He gained legal right to this world to mar humans with his character and image when they forfeited their dominion. It was Satan's plan to trap the Savior in the flesh during His mission on Earth as an offspring of humanity; the same plan he enacted with our first parents. Yet, Satan failed to kill Jesus as a baby and tried to trap Him by false worship.[13] Only by prayer and fasting was our Savior able to overcome the consistent attacks and temptations on His life and character. Had Satan been successful, Christ would have been recreated as Satan's offspring, contradicting the Savior's own creation that He came to save.

---

[13] Mt. 2:16

Satan failed at taking the throne of God in heaven by force. He had to release an alternate plan to tempt Jesus to take on his image by sinning. Had he succeeded, Satan would have been able to accuse God of being wrong and himself right. He would have been able to call himself god because he would have proven that no one could live by God's law—not even God Himself. If God is ever wrong, God will cease to be God. If Christ had given into any temptation, He would have forfeited being God, taken on the image of Satan, and we would have been forever enslaved to sin. Satan accused the Savior of not being able to keep His law and tried his hardest to get Him to break it. If he had gained this advantage over Jesus, Christ would have conformed to the image of Satan which would have allowed Satan to be a god. God would bear the enemy's image, following the pattern of Adam and Eve. But Christ did not fail. He overcame everything for us.

We are given two clear examples of how to overcome sin. We see it through the scriptures about the earthly high priests who prayed with clean hands in the Most Holy Place on the Day of Atonement. We see how Christ, our High Priest, prays for us now. Christ gained the right to continuously intercede for us because of His victory. He can pray us through every stage of a battle with sin because He prayed through every stage of His battle with sin into victory. Romans 8:34 tells us that He has done it all for us. He has lived our life, died, and now is at the right hand of the Father interceding for us. Coming to Him in prayer lets Him live in us by the power of the Holy Spirit, which is the only way that we can overcome as He did.

The Holy Spirit is God and knows what is in our hearts just as He knew the heart of Christ when He was fighting His flesh. Christ lived with a human heart while also being God; He knows what's in our heart. Through the Holy Spirit, He searches out the things in our hearts that we need to change and gives us freedom. The Holy Spirit convicts us of those things and leads us in prayer according to the will of God. It was the Holy Spirit that caused the groans from our Savior as He prayed when He was weak. When we come to God in our weakness and ask for help, the Holy Spirit will pray those same groans for us the way He did for Christ.[14] You do not have to fight this battle alone. Jesus is more than able and willing to do in us what we cannot do for ourselves. God can convict us to do what we don't want to do or show us the sin we love and don't want to stop; He will help us to want what is right. Ask Christ to fight your battles for you.

---

[14] Rm. 8:27 and Hb. 5:7

Reflection Questions

➤ What kind of prayers did Christ pray to overcome?

➤ What prayers does Christ pray now as High Priest?

➤ What is the power that kept Christ from sinning that the Father wants to give to us?

➤ What standard did Jesus live by and fulfill for us?

➤ What was Satan's sole purpose for tempting Christ?

➤ What does Romans 8:34 tell us?

Personal Prayer

• What will the Holy Spirit do for us?

• Write a heartfelt prayer based on what you have learned in today's reading.

_____

_____

_____

_____

_____

_____

_____

_____

_____

_____

_____

_____

_____

_____

_____

DAY FOUR

Passing Through

"Since then we have a great high priest who has passed through the heavens, Jesus, the Son of God, let us hold fast our confession."
—*Hebrews 4:14 (ESV)*

Living a victorious life in Christ is simple, but it is not always easy. Many times, we may ask ourselves, *"Is eternity with God worth all of the hardship we experience in life on Earth?"* To help us experience the benefits of life with Him, God blesses us with the support of others during our time here. Through communities and their encouragement, we are able to endure the rough times of our Christian walk. Yet, all too often we feel alone, as if we don't have the support of others. God designed our walk with Him to develop us in this way. He wants us to know Him as His Son came to know Him.

God wants to be our refuge from trouble and our true comfort. Yes, He gives us community with other believers to help us grow in our Christian walk, but ultimately it is in Him where we find our strength and help. While human beings can be companions, they cannot be the *way* for us to walk. Other believers may be excellent examples of Christ-likeness, praying for us and caring for us, but they are not and cannot be our *way* of living and praying. Christ alone is our example and we can only be fulfilled in Him.

Christ says in John 14:6, *"I am the way, the truth and the life. No one comes to the Father, but by me."* The way that Christ walked this life by prayer is the only way that we can come to the Father. He understands everything we have been through and will go through because He has been through everything for us. Philippians 2:6-8 says, *"Who though he existed in the form of God did not regard equality with God as something to be grasped, but emptied himself by taking on the form of a slave, by looking like other men, and by sharing in human nature. He humbled himself, by becoming obedient to the point of death – even death on a cross."* No other human has been through every trial and experienced every weakness as Christ.

Christ may have experienced temptations that we have not because He was fully human and fully God. 1 Corinthians 10:13, says, *"No temptation has overtaken you that is not common to man."* In addition to every common temptation known to man, Christ may have faced and dealt with things that no one else has because of His uncommon nature as God and man. He bore and overcame much more than what the human mind can comprehend or realize today. Through His nature, Christ provides a way of escape for us. He is our *way* of escape by being changed through daily prayer in the presence God. God is faithful and He will not let us be tempted beyond what we can handle. Gracefully, He provides us with strength and a way of escape so we may endure.

Hebrews 4:14-15 tells us that Christ was able to go back to heaven and intercede as High Priest for us because of His victory on Earth. In order to take the journey back to heaven as High Priest, Jesus had to walk the journey of life prayerfully. Moment by moment and day to day.

In verse 14, the word for *passed through* is *dierchomai.* In this text, it specifically means "to travel the road which leads through a place; go, pass, travel through a region."[15] This is important to note because Christ's prayer life was a journey to His death and resurrection.

---

15 Joseph Thayer, Thayer's Greek Lexicon,
https://biblehub.com/greek/1330.htm, (2011)

Passing through something indicates a process taking place. Christ did not teleport to His victory. It was something He had to walk out. His faith walk to death and resurrection was a process for Him just as it is for us. The Holy Spirit takes us on this walk when we unite with Him. He gives us the life of Christ to live out the journey of faith by prayer, which allows us to overcome; the same way He did with Christ. The Holy Spirit led Jesus into the wilderness where the enemy tried to tempt Him.[16] Only by the power of the Holy Spirit was Jesus able to sustain His connection to the Father. Likewise, the Holy Spirit will lead us through this life as He did with Christ.

Jesus walked the road to the cross by His continual, prayerful connection to the Father. He was able to pass from death to life so He could later pass through the heavens to continually intercede for us. Jesus successfully trekked the earth so He could travel back to heaven a victor over sin, possessing all authority. He did this so we can do it. Just as *dierchomai* reflects Christ's journey, so it reflects our salvific journey through the life of Christ that allows us access to the throne of grace.[17] Our walk on Earth must be like His, so our journey into heaven can be like His.

Do you feel tired in this journey? At times, do you feel incapable of walking as Jesus did? If so, don't be discouraged. God is eagerly waiting to empower you by the Holy Spirit. Christ wants to live in you to help you do what you can't do on your own. Ask Him to walk this journey out through you so you can walk in the victory that has been made available to you.

---

[16] Lk. 4:1-13
[17] Hb. 4:16

Reflection Questions

➢ Why has God designed the Christian walk to feel lonely at times?

➢ Explain why we must look to Christ, instead of other believers, as our ultimate example of a relationship with God?

➢ What is provided to us to overcome temptation and why?

Personal Prayer

• Explain the meaning of the word *dierchomai* in our life as it relates to Christ.

• Write a heartfelt prayer based on what you learned from today's reading.

_____

_____

_____

_____

_____

_____

_____

_____

_____

_____

_____

_____

_____

DAY
FIVE

Defining Sin

"For we do not have a high priest who is unable to sympathize with our weaknesses, but one who in every respect has been tempted as we are, yet without sin."

—*Hebrews 4:15 (ESV)*

Christ lived without sinning. We know this because of the record of His life. How often do we read the word of God and think to ourselves, "How did He live without sinning a single day in His life? How did He overcome the temptations presented to Him?" When we think of sin, we tend to think of actions; typically, offenses committed towards God or another human. But what is sin, truly? What does it mean that Christ lived without giving into any of the weaknesses that He bore on our behalf? It is important to fundamentally understand what sin is so we can understand how Christ did not sin.

The New Testament uses the word sin in several different contexts. The word for *sin* in Hebrews 4:15 is *hamartia,* with the original definition in Hebrew meaning "to miss the mark." *Hamartia* originally conveyed the idea of missing the mark as when hunting with a bow and arrow and then missing or falling short of any goal, standard, or purpose."[18] It is also used to describe an offense. In the same verse in Hebrews, it is used to illustrate how Christ lived a life without committing any kind of offense in word, thought, or action. The word *hamartia* stems from the word *meros* which means "a part, share of," and has the prefix *a* meaning *not.* These two together mean "no share,"

---

[18] Bruce Hurt, Preceptaustin.org. Bruce Hurt, http://www.preceptaustin.org/romans 520-21.htm#s, (accessed 10/9/18)

"no part of" loss or forfeiture because of not hitting the target. *Hamartia* is also defined as "self-originated or self-empowered nature; not originated or empowered by God."[19]

Having learned the various definitions of *sin,* how can we apply them to the description of Christ's walk?

It's interesting that the word for *sin* comes from a word that means "not sharing in, no part of, loss or forfeiture." What would a person have to lack in order for sin to take place in them? The answer is the divine nature of God. It's the same nature Adam and Eve were created with but forfeited when they chose to eat fruit from the Tree of the Knowledge of Good and Evil. Adam and Eve no longer shared the same nature as their Creator. They forfeited their divine nature by listening to the lies of Satan, opting to share in his nature. This caused a broken relationship with their Creator. Eve started to share Satan's thoughts when he questioned her about God's command about eating from the tree. She started doubting. When Eve did this, she gave up the mind of God for the mind of Satan. This was the type of doubtful thinking that caused Satan's fall as well. He began doubting the authority of God's word and reasoned that what He said was not the truth. Eve doubted because as Satan shared his thoughts with her, she believed them and took on his mindset. This began humanity's sin. Adam and Eve forfeited the mind of God for the mind of Satan which led to their offense of eating the fruit. They lost their righteousness; their right-standing with God resulting in their broken relationship with God and one another.[20] This caused the condition of sin.

When Christ was on Earth and lived without sin, He chose

---

19 Gleason Archer and Gary Hill, Helps Word-Studies, https://biblehub.com/greek/266.htm, (2011)
20 Gn. 3

not to listen to the lies the enemy presented to Him. When someone believes a lie of Satan, it causes a broken relationship with God, which leads to the action of offense we call sin. A fleshy mind is an offense to God.[21] Christ chose not to forfeit His divine thinking to the enemy no matter how hard-pressed He was to do so. It would have caused a broken relationship with His Father and that would have been sin. He maintained a consistent exchange of thoughts between Him and the Father so He would not fall. Christ's connection with the Father was constant so that His share in the divine nature would not be tainted by the nature of Satan.

We experience sin when we have no share in God's divine nature. Sin was the result of the fall in the Garden of Eden that resulted in a broken relationship with God for all of humanity. Our sin nature is what leads us to commit offensive actions. However, Christ's life, death and resurrection repaired that breach for us. He is our reconciliation.[22] He did not give into the temptation that would lead to a forfeited relationship so that we may reclaim ours.

---

[21] 2 Pt. 1:4; Rm. 8:7
[22] 2 Co. 5:18

Reflection Questions

➢ What does the word *hamartia* mean in relation to sin?

➢ How is it used to describe Christ's walk in today's verse?

➢ What did Adam and Eve forfeit by listening to the serpent and eating the forbidden fruit?

➢ What does Romans 8:7 tell us about the mind?

➢ What was the key to Christ maintaining His relationship with the Father?

➢ What has been made available to us because of Christ?

Personal Prayer

Write a heartfelt, personal prayer based on what you learned in today's reading.

_____

_____

_____

_____

_____

_____

_____

_____

_____

_____

_____

_____

_____

_____

DAY
SIX

Christ, Our Reconciliation

"For every high priest chosen from among men is appointed to act on behalf of men in relation to God, to offer gifts and sacrifices for sins."
—*Hebrews 5:1 (ESV)*

The ceremonial practices of the Old Testament were completely fulfilled by the crucifixion of Christ. Jesus is High Priest. He is the offered gift. He is the sacrifice and He became sin. All that is needed for our reconciliation to the Father is found in Christ. Paul says in 2 Corinthians 5:21, *"For our sake he made him to be sin who knew no sin, so that in him we might become the righteousness of God,"* and Ephesians 5:2, *"Christ loved us and gave himself up for us as a fragrant offering and sacrifice to God."*

The high priest of the Old Testament offered a sacrifice for His own sin and for the people of Israel. This was symbolic of the sacrifice Christ would make. Though He was sinless, when Christ died, He became sin and His sacrifice was made on behalf of humanity. He became what we are—sin, living in a broken relationship with God, so that we can become what He is—righteousness, which is right-standing with God.[23]

When Christ was on the cross and asked the Father, *"Why have you left me?"* He became illustrative of the impact and severity of sin.[24] In becoming sin, Christ surrendered to God what separated us from God. Sin is the brokenness of our relationship with God that caused us to forfeit God's divine character.[25] The Greek word for the phrase *"have you forsaken*

---

[23] 1 Co. 5:21
[24] Mt. 27:45
[25] Mt. 27:46; When Eve first made the choice to receive the serpent's advice it was sin before she ate the fruit. This caused a breach between her

me" is *egkataleípō*. It means, "left in a condition of lack; helpless; in dire circumstances; to leave behind."[26] Although Jesus never sinned, He became sin and while on the cross, experienced the lack of His Father's divine character. He was left with feeling only His humanness although He was fully human and fully God. What He experienced was the inherent lack of our sinful condition; the lack of connection to the Father.

When He asked, *"Why have you left me?"* it expressed His feelings of devastation from the blow of feeling separated from His Father; the Father had kept Him and helped Him maintain His connection during His life on Earth. Christ lived out what we had prior to the fall; a constant connection with the Father. Through His walk, subsequent death, and resurrection, He reestablished the constant connection with the Father for humanity.

Jesus felt as if the Father had left Him when He was experiencing the void of a breached relationship with the Father caused by sin. This condition was invited into human existence when Adam and Eve sinned by eating the forbidden fruit. They were separated from God because they turned from Him and disobeyed the boundaries He set.

Since Jesus is God incarnate, it was the conflict in His soul that caused Him to cry out, *"Why have you forsaken me?"* He felt the strain of His divinity clinging to His Father while His human side was leaving the Father. He felt as if God left Him,

---

and God before she even realized it. She exchanged godly desires for evil ones; thus, changing her character. Christ has given us a principle teaching in Mt. 5:27-28, that if we even think on and desire to do something that is wrong, we have already sinned before the action is carried out.

[26] James Strong, Strong's Concordance, http://biblehub.com/greek/1459.htm, (1905) and Gleason Archer and Gary Hill, Helps Word-Studies, http://bible.hub.com/greek/1459.htm, (2011)

even though He didn't. He experienced man leaving God and the impact of a broken relationship. Sin makes us feel as if God has left man when instead it is man who has left God.

While Jesus walked the earth, He warred with His flesh and battled temptations to disconnect from His Father. Christ did not know what it was like to be without the Father or to sin. He had only experienced the temptation of the disconnect up to that point. Now, Jesus has become it.

The feeling of Him becoming sin made Him feel as if God left Him. Yes, God did pour out His wrath on Christ as a means to destroy humanity's sin, which Christ bore.[27] But, Christ also divinely surrendered to the Father's will to take on humanity's sin, fulfilling His purpose on Earth. The Father promised to bring an end to sin by destroying the chasm it caused, even at the expense of the feeling of disconnection from His beloved Son.[28]

What Christ experienced in His being when He became sin is complex. Though the Father never left Him, Christ experienced banishment to hell: the hell that those who decide not to be saved will experience.[29]

---

[27] The word for wrath in this context of the Greek language is orgé. It means "swelling up to constitutionally oppose; properly, settled anger (i.e. rising up from an ongoing (fixed) opposition); proceeds from an internal disposition which steadfastly opposes someone, or something based on extended personal exposure, i.e. solidifying what the beholder considers wrong (unjust, evil); It is not a sudden outburst, but rather (referring to God's) fixed, controlled, passionate feeling against sin . . . a settled indignation." God's wrath poured out on Christ as a sacrifice is a final solution for all evil. It was not something to condemn, punish, or torture His Son, in effort to satisfy a vindictive anger. But it was to extinguish sin that is opposingly offensive to the nature of God and humanity's state before the fall. Since Jesus became sin, He received sin's consequences as an act of love.

[28] Rm. 5:8-9

[29] Rm. 2:8-9

Hell is eternal separation from God. What Christ felt was not the Father's heart towards Him but the eternal separation from God because He had taken on sin. Although He felt forsaken by His Father, He wasn't. The Father was keeping His promise. He had to do it. This was the first time God the Son was separated from God the Father. So, while the Father never left Him, His wrath was poured out on Christ as a representative of all who decide to remain apart from God. Christ clung to the Father as He experienced feelings of abandonment. Jesus felt abandoned and forsaken, while the Father saw His actions fulfill the desires of those who do not choose eternal life. Christ becoming sin was in conflict with the relationship He had established with the Father. Christ's divine desire to never leave God was weighted against the human nature of temptation and sin He became. It's as if Christ said, *"I've done everything right. Why have you left me?"* Yet, separation and reconciliation took place within Christ on the cross. When the final blow of death came to the breach, reconciliation bridged the chasm by the body of Christ.

The cross was death's final blow after what had taken place during His walk when He wrestled and confessed. The tension was finally laid to rest so the connection Jesus established while incarnate could thrive without interference from the flesh. Broken relationship with God and reconciliation both took place in His body. Life and death both took place in Christ. He is our death and life. He is humanity's reconciliation. As the broken relationship received its deadly blow, righteousness was allowed to live in us. Jesus put on the flesh, filled with works of death, and destroyed sin. Now, we can put on His righteousness and experience right-standing with God.

Jesus also became the experience every believer will go through who chooses to die in Him. Jesus died, holding to the hope that the sacrifice of His life and death would meet His Father's approval and reunite them. The enemy tried to lie to Jesus. He told Him this was the end and there was no hope. Satan tried to convince Christ of the eternal grip of death and make Him believe He would not be reunited with His Father. Every believer who dies in Christ can have His experience when they are on their deathbed, clinging to the promises of God. The enemy will be there to taunt with the lie that death is eternal, but they must not give in. Like Christ, they must cling to the promises of God in Jesus.

Jesus had a final breakthrough while on the cross. He received assurance He had conquered eternal death and the death of those that would die in Him. In that moment, a peace came to Him and He said, *"It is finished."*[30] He knew His Father never left Him and eternal separation and eternal reconciliation had been fulfilled in His body at once. Likewise, those who die in Jesus can experience peace, knowing what God has worked out for them is complete. God will not leave His believers, even as they battle to their last breath.

---

[30] Jn. 19:28-30

Reflection Questions

➤ What are the three things Christ fulfilled in Himself according to Hebrews 5:1?

➤ What does *egkataleipō* mean?

➤ What was destroyed in the body of Christ?

➤ In your own words, describe the experience of Christ while on the cross.

➤ What was fulfilled for unbelievers?

➤ What was fulfilled for believers?

Personal Prayer

Write a heartfelt prayer of gratitude, thanking Jesus for what He did on the cross.

_____

_____

_____

_____

_____

_____

_____

_____

_____

_____

_____

_____

_____

_____

DAY SEVEN

The Nature of Christ

"For we do not have a high priest who is unable to sympathize with our weaknesses, but one who in every respect has been tempted as we are, yet without sin."

—Hebrews 4:15 (ESV)

Hebrews 4:15 exemplifies the central tenet of the nature of Christ. The verse shows His divine ability to help us live the life of freedom He offers. There is so much theological writing and religious debate about what Christ's nature was during His life on Earth. Many scholars believe He had a pre-lapsarian nature, which is the belief that His nature was of man before sin entered the world. Others claim He had a post-lapsarian nature, which is the belief that His nature was of man after sin entered the world. These terms come from the Latin word *lapsus,* meaning "to slip or fall."[31]

While understanding the nature of Christ is important, the simplistic beauty of Christ's experience with every struggle and temptation humans face can get lost in the arguments. Yes, He was God incarnate. He came to Earth as God and man in one. Despite the studies about His nature, we only have a surface understanding without a joint fellowship in His experience. Only an experiential knowledge of what He went through for us can help us understand His nature on deeper levels.

Christ was God restoring humanity back to its divine state before sin entered the world. Man had a divine nature before sin because man walked with God and shared His nature. We

---

[31] Merriam-Webster, s.v. "pre-lapsarian", accessed February 1, 2018, https://www.merriam-webster.com/dictionary/prelapsarian.

lost that after sin. Christ's nature was an integration of His divine perfection and our sinful tendencies. Even with the experience that He calls humanity into with Him, we will never fully understand His nature because we have not had every experience that He has had. As mentioned in Day 5, Jesus has experienced every weakness that every human ever has. However, we identify with Him in His sufferings and in His divine nature.[32] [The Apostle] Paul tells us to no longer regard Christ to the flesh.[33] He calls us into an experience with Him that allows us to walk by His Spirit, by which He overcame sin and death.

The most important thing for us to understand about the nature of Christ is He identified with us in the flesh so we can identify with Him in the Spirit. Hebrews 4:15 uses the word *sumpatheo* in the Greek to define how Christ identified with us. It means "to experience pain jointly or of some kind." In the context of the verse, the definition includes "having compassion based on the experience of the joint pain."[34] It translates in English to the word *sympathize,* which means "caring and understanding for the suffering of others."

Not only does Christ *sympathize* with us, He also *empathizes* with us. *Empathy,* which is often used interchangeably with *sympathy,* means "the ability to experience the feelings of another." The only way someone can experience someone else's feelings is to have walked in their shoes. Verse 15 tells us that Christ was tempted in *"every respect"* that we are tempted. The phrase *"every respect"* translates from the Greek to mean,

---

[32] Pp. 3:10
[33] 2. Co. 5:16
[34] Bruce Hurt, Preceptaustin.org. Bruce Hurt, http://www.preceptaustin.org/hebrews_415.htm#s, (accessed 10/9/18)

"all, every; all things."[35] He faced every sinful temptation and hardship that humans face and overcame them all, according to the word of God.

Christ experienced weakness as we do. The word for weakness in the Greek is *astheneia* meaning "without strength; refers to an ailment that deprives someone of enjoying or accomplishing what they would like to do; focuses on the handicaps that go with the weakness."[36] This definition shows we have no strength to do right, even if we want to, because of sin. We are handicapped of any strength of our own, and Christ experienced that for us. He lived without exercising His own divine strength so He could rely on the Holy Spirit to impart grace to Him to overcome temptation. Christ cannot give us something He did not receive. He can give us grace because He lived by grace while here on Earth. He relied on the Holy Spirit for grace and power. When He was weak, the power of God's divine nature was made perfect in Him to help Him overcome. [The Apostle Paul] says in 2 Corinthians 12:9, *"But he said to me, 'My grace is sufficient for you, for my power is made perfect in weakness.' Therefore, I will boast all the more gladly of my weaknesses, so that the power of Christ may rest upon me."* Paul understood the power of Christ to keep him from falling. He experienced Christ in weakness and in strength, as Christ experienced how His Father kept Him by the power of the Holy Spirit. God wants that for each of us too.

No matter what sin or hardship you deal with, be it lack of love, anger, pride, jealousy, greed, sexual perversion, identity issues, hopelessness, depression, suicidal thoughts or feelings,

---

[35] James Strong, Strong's Concordance, https://biblehub.com/greek/3956.htm, (1905) and Bible Hub, https://biblehub.com/text/hebrews/4-15.htm, (accessed 10/9/18)

[36] Gleason Archer and Gary Hill, Helps Word- Studies, https://biblehub.com/greek/769.htm, (2011)

addiction, rejection, self-hatred, unforgiveness and all others, Christ has been touched with those weakness. He has overcome them, and He wants to give you the grace and power to overcome as well. Will you ask Him to do it for you?

Reflection Questions

➢ Based on today's reading, what is the primary facet we need to understand about Christ? How does it relate to us?

➢ Describe the nature of Christ in simple words.

➢ What did Christ gain by experiencing our weaknesses?

➢ What do we gain by joint fellowship in His walk?

➢ What was the ultimate goal of Christ's walk?

➢ What does the word *sumpatheo* mean?

➢ Explain why the meaning of *sumpatheo* is important to your relationship with Christ.

➢ What temptations did Christ experience and how many is He able to help us overcome?

➢ From where did Christ draw His strength?

Personal Prayer

Write a personal, heartfelt prayer based on what you learned today and pray it.

_____

_____

_____

_____

_____

_____

_____

_____

DAY
EIGHT

Christ's Fight with His Flesh

"In the days of his flesh, Jesus offered up prayers and supplications, with loud cries and tears, to him who was able to save him from death, and he was heard because of his reverence."

—*Hebrews 5:7 (ESV)*

Jesus went through so much during His earthly mission. It is difficult to comprehend the spiritual, emotional, and mental hardships He endured as He overcame sin. His prayer life was marked by pain and anguish. As believers, we can go through hard times that cause us great anguish and drive us to the brink of tears, but none of us have wrestled with our flesh to the same extent as Christ. He suffered much and, in most times, endured physical distress in ways we can only begin to fathom.[37]

Hebrews 5:7 says, *"In the days of his flesh, Jesus offered up prayers and supplications, with loud cries and tears, to him who was able to save him from death, and he was heard because of his reverence."* How many times can we say we wrestled with our sinful tendencies, causing us to cry out as He did? We may have cried out to God after suffering the consequences of our sin or because of a painful experience. There are also times we may have petitioned God and cried because we were hard-pressed due to temptation or attacks from the enemy. The type of cry Jesus cried, however, outweighs the cry of any human.

1 Corinthians 10:13 tells us there is no temptation uncommon to man that we cannot bear or that God will not provide a way of escape. He will help us endure it or flee from

---

[37] Hb. 12:3-4

it. Think about your biggest temptation, whether it be a current struggle or past experience. Know there are others who deal with the same thing because it's common to man. We can identify with them and they with us. Jesus, on the other hand, wrestled in a way no human would be able to fully identify because He was God and man.

There are people who have suffered much for Christ, but we as individuals will never suffer from everything He did in the way He did. He wrestled with every common temptation and probably faced uncommon frustrations from the enemy that we have not experienced because He is God.

The word *cries* in the Greek language is *kraugé*. It means "an outcry, done with great emotion; clamorous screaming and shrieking that is extremely boisterous. Like a wounded person emitting non-human types of sounds."[38] Christ's outcry is described as loud in the original language. Isn't an outcry intrinsically loud? Why then is an outcry, with an inherent definition of being loud, described again as loud? The double emphasis exists for a reason. *Loud* is defined as "strong and mighty" in this text by the word *ischuros*.[39] It is derived from an adjective that means "engaging in combative strength."

These types of cries were a result of Christ's flesh going through the process of dying to sin for us. He received wounds to the carnal man from death blows to our nature. The Holy Spirit was putting to death our carnal nature in His flesh. His cries were for the mighty strength that can only come by the Holy Spirit in weakness. 2 Corinthians 12:8-10 tells us, *"God's strength is made perfect in our weakness."* On the cross, the Holy

---

[38] Gleason Archer and Gary Hill, Helps Word-Studies, https://biblehub.com/greek/2906.htm, (2011)
[39] Gleason Archer and Gary Hill, Helps Word-Studies, https://biblehub.com/greek/2478.htm, (2011)

Spirit warred against humankind's carnal nature causing Jesus to cry for help to His Father the way He did. He did not rely on His own strength but on the power given to Him by His Father through the Spirit.

As He cried out to the Father during the process, Christ had faith and knew the Father could keep Him from giving in to temptation, thereby choosing eternal death. The word for *death* in the text is *thánatos* and it can refer to a physical or spiritual death.[40] Figuratively speaking, death can mean separation from the life *(salvation)* of God forever by dying without first experiencing death to self; the requirement to receive His gift of salvation. By the time He was crucified, our carnal man that Christ put on was already dead because of His process of daily dying. The same process He went through, we go through in Him.[41] The prayer and supplications Christ uttered with "loud cries and tears" were for the strength He needed to rely on His Father to overcome. The word for *prayer* in this verse expresses Jesus praying for a specific, deep, heartfelt, and personal need stemming from a sense of lack.[42] *Supplications* are described as "earnest asking or begging for peace, relief and reconciliation."[43] Christ cried out for the strength that we would need to overcome and for our peace and reconciliation with the Father. This can only come by death to our carnal man and subsequent receipt of the nature of Christ. All of this was done by His reverent submission to His Father.

---

[40] Gleason Archer and Gary Hill, Helps Word-Studies, https://biblehub.com/greek/2288.htm, (2011)

[41] 1. Co. 15:31

[42] Gleason Archer and Gary Hill, Helps Word-Studies, https://biblehub.com/greek/1162.htm, (2011)

[43] Gleason Archer and Gary Hill, Helps Word-Studies, https://biblehub.com/greek/2428.htm, (2011)

We are called into the same experience to overcome as Christ was; just as He obligated Himself to our experience. He faced the temptations of lust of the flesh and eyes as well as the pride of life in the wilderness. In Gethsemane, He was tempted to give up and abandon the process. He identified with us in the flesh so that we may identify with Him in the Spirit.[44] He faced the temptations we face and more. Christ overcame them all so we can have His experience in the Spirit.

Reflection Questions

> To what extent did Jesus experience anguish in overcoming sin?
> Name the four temptations of Christ mentioned in today's reading.
> How do you think Jesus identifies with you in your battles with temptation?
> How does understanding what Christ experienced help you identify with Him more?
> How does today's reading encourage you in your relationship with God?

Personal Prayer

Write a heartfelt, personal prayer asking God to help you identify with Christ the way He identifies with you.

_____

_____

_____

_____

_____

[44] 2 Co. 5:16 and Rm. 8:9

DAY
NINE

How He Learned Obedience

"Although he was a son, he learned obedience through what he suffered. And being made perfect, he became the source of eternal salvation to all who obey him."

—Hebrews 5:8-9 (ESV)

If your child asked you to do something that was torturous to them... in an attempt to help others... who have no cognizance of being in need of help, and a majority of them may not even want to receive the help once it is brought to their awareness....

Would you do it?

I don't think too many parents would immediately jump to fulfill this request or do it at all. They might even have their child mentally evaluated.

Nevertheless, this is what Jesus and our Heavenly Father did for us. Jesus and the Father wanted to rescue humanity from the consequences of sin. They did not want us to suffer eternal consequences, so They decided on a plan to save us before we knew we needed saving.

Although Christ was chosen and obligated by His Father, He became our sacrifice through personal desire and choice.[45] The Father loves us as much as He loves Jesus.[46] Granting Jesus' request aligned with God's will. They are one and wanted to restore us and make us one with Them again.

Jesus poses the question in Matthew 7:9-10, *"Which one of you, if his son asks him for bread, will give him a stone? Or if he asks for*

---

[45] Jn. 17:24
[46] Jn. 17:22-23

a fish, will give him a serpent?" No one is the answer! Parents love their children and want the best for them so they can be happy. Parents want to give their children what is pleasurable to them; not subject them to discomfort. That would be sadistic.

It is a mystery why Jesus chose to suffer the way He did for us. What He asked the Father for was difficult to achieve, but the end result was what mattered. When He asked the Father to give humanity to Him, He knew what would be necessary to receive us.

Christ suffered greatly. In the eyes of an unbeliever, it may look like Jesus asked the Father for bread or a fish and instead He received a stone or serpent. Hebrews 12:2 clarifies how Jesus died for the joy that was set before Him. The joy He saw was humanity coming into a relationship of willful and submissive obedience to the Father as a result of what He suffered for us. If God the Father had not granted Christ's request, they would not have been on one accord. It would have been as if God was giving Christ a stone instead of bread.

Hebrews 5:8 says, *"He learned obedience by what he suffered."* The paradox of this truth is that Jesus never did anything wrong. Have you ever heard of the saying, "A hard head makes a soft behind"? This means if you are not obedient by listening to instruction, you'll learn as you suffer the consequences of disobedience. That is the redicament of sin. Jesus never sinned but he learned obedience for us as if He had through His suffering.

The word for *learned* in this verse means "an accustomed habit by use and practice that causes one to learn." The word for *obedience* means "submission to what is heard; the response to someone speaking."[47] Jesus learned to practice listening

---

[47] Gleason Archer and Gary Hill, Helps Word-Studies, https://biblehub.com/greek/5218.htm, (2011)

because of His suffering, even though He never committed sin. He was learning in our place. He learned to obey as if He hadn't properly listened. He brought the afflictions of His flesh to His Father and surrendered them so His obedience would be made perfect. He suffered for us so He can help us through this walk and not have to deal with the eternal consequences of sin.

Loving parents have a difficult time disciplining their children; it causes them more pain than the kids. Yet, parents know they are responsible for teaching important lessons through discipline so their children can avoid having to learn harsher lessons later in life.

Christ tells us in Matthew 7:11, *"If you who are evil know how to give good gifts to your children, why do we think that the Father would withhold anything good from us?"* We didn't even ask for Jesus but the Father still gave us everything good in Him. Why? He loves us with a love so rich, no one can fully comprehend it. The Father granted His Son's request so He could overcome our sin through suffering and dying our death.

When we see our need for a life of obedience to the Father and ask Him for it, the *Good Thing* He gives us is Jesus by the power of His Holy Spirit. Christ's suffering did not feel good to Him, but it was good for us. His suffering accomplished its purpose: reconciliation with God. His suffering is what we need. We must identify with Jesus in the Spirit to have the good gift of salvation offered in Him. We must also learn obedience through the sufferings of Christ. When we ask to be obedient like Christ, we are asking for His experience so we can share in His life.[48]

Jesus, the Father and the Holy Spirit do not want us to experience the discomfort of suffering eternal consequences

---

[48] 2 Co. 5:16, Rm. 8:9,17

for our sin. They decided Christ would take on our suffering and allow us to experience eternal bliss, if we choose. Being reunited with Them, face-to-face, in Their Kingdom is God's best plan for us.

Reflection Questions

➢ Based on today's reading, briefly explain the motivation for Christ's self-sacrifice.
➢ How did Jesus learn obedience?
➢ How does understanding how Christ learned obedience impact your relationship with Him?
➢ Based on today's reading, how are we to relate to Christ?

Personal Prayer

Write a heartfelt prayer asking God to help you grow in your devotion to Him and how to identify with Christ.

_____

_____

_____

_____

_____

_____

_____

_____

_____

_____

_____

_____

His Perfecting for Our Perfection

"Although he was a son, he learned obedience through what he suffered. And being made perfect, he became the source [author] of eternal salvation to all who obey him." *

—Hebrews 5:8-9 (ESV)

Jesus had to become who we are *and* who He has destined us to be to save us and take us into our destiny with Him. He had to go through the process to be changed. He endured *"being made perfect"* for us. Philippians 2:5-11 gives us a picture of Christ's process. He had to humble Himself completely. He became a servant and was obedient to the point of death. He fully relied on His Father. He took no thought of His own. Though He was God, and could have used His power for Himself, He did not exploit it. Had Jesus used His power to His advantage at any point during His time on Earth, it would have been a direct contradiction to His purpose. He purposefully surrendered in obedience to the will of God for salvation to come through Him. Had He used His own power for Himself, it would have been a form of self-righteous works which would have led to death.[49] This would have caused relational incongruence with His Father and set a standard for man to live independent of God while still reaping the benefits of salvation.

The example would suggest that humans could save themselves by their own works. We cannot. We have no power

---

[49] Rm. 10:3,4

of our own. The power we do have is given to us by God. Though Christ was fully God and fully human and able to use the power of His divinity for Himself, He surrendered the use of His power to the Father and depended on Him for strength. Likewise, any power that we have, we are to live in submission to the Father.

Christ went through the process of living humbly and in full surrender to the Father and won the battle for us. The phrase *"being made perfect"* translates from the Greek word *teleioó* meaning "to bring to an end, complete, working through the entire process, perfect." The root word *tel-* means, "reaching the end aim."[50] The root is important because we often work through processes and never quite hit the mark. We continue to try until we reach the desired result, or we give up. Our Savior worked through the process of humility and suffered without committing sin. He perfected and sealed our salvation in Him. While we can make mistakes, He could not. The enemy claimed no one could live and be sinless before God. But Jesus did it! He did it for us! He became perfect so we can be perfected in Him.

An extension of the definition for *"being made perfect"* is "to raise to the state befitting him; God exalting Jesus to the state of heavenly majesty."[51] The only way Jesus could be exalted was to humble Himself. Philippians 2:10-11 tells us that God has given Him a name above all other names and everyone will bow and worship Him at the mention of it. Christ's form of servanthood was meant to exalt Him and provide restoration for us. Christ bore the flesh and image of a fallen man, but that

---

[50] Gleason Archer and Gary Hill, Helps Word-Studies, https://biblehub.com/greek/5048.htm, (2011)
[51] Joseph Thayer, Thayer's Greek Lexicon, https://biblehub.com/greek/5048.htm, (2011)

was not humanity's original state. Man was made in God's image and as the Father exalted Jesus after being made perfect, He wanted to do the same for us. He wants to perfect and restore us through humility, so He can exalt us and change our name.[52]

The word for *became* in the original language is *ginomai* and it is used to describe how Christ became our High Priest. It describes "emerging, becoming or transitioning from one point, realm or condition to another." It describes God's emergence from eternity and becoming (showing Themselves) in time (physical space). *Ginomai* describes a change in Christ's role and physical position from earthly intercessor to Heavenly High Priest. In Hebrews 5:9, *ginomai* describes a transitional fulfillment, the completion of Christ's work, and His state of being. He became the source of our salvation and new life. *Salvation* defines God's rescue as two-fold; it delivers believers out of destruction and into His safety and gives us His life when we accept salvation.[53]

Jesus became like us when He exited eternity and entered time and space. He became perfect then exited time and returned to eternity. We must become like Him and follow Him into eternity. We must humble ourselves and become obedient to have eternal life. He is the example of how we are to work out our salvation. Philippians 2:12 gives us Christ's blueprint for salvation. We are told we must *"work out our salvation with fear and trembling."* The scripture describes people who distrust their ability to meet all requirements and surrender their all to fulfill their duty to God. Just as Jesus was a servant and intercessor, we are to be also. Just as He is our

---

[52] Rv. 3:12 and 3:21
[53] Gleason Archer and Gary Hill, Helps Word-Studies, https://biblehub.com/greek/1096.htm, (2011)

Eternal Life, so are we to live with Him throughout eternity.

He *"became the author [source] of our salvation"* and we have eternal life in Him. In this instance, *author* means "that in which the cause of anything resides." Jesus is the person of the Godhead who created us. Life was given through Him at creation.[54] New life comes through Him by restoration.[55] He is the one who seals our eternal life by His salvation.[56]

Reflection Questions

- ➤ Why did Jesus have to rely on the Father and how does this set an example for us in our relationship with God?
- ➤ What is the difference between Christ's personal process and ours?
- ➤ Does understanding Christ's process bring you encouragement? If so, how?
- ➤ What outcome does the Father expect from our process?
- ➤ Describe the difference between salvation and life.
- ➤ In your own words, explain what Philippians 2:12 teaches us.
- ➤ How do you see Philippians 2:12 as an example of Christ's process?

---

[54] Jn. 1:1-3 and Hb. 1:1-2; James Strong, Strong's Concordance, https://biblehub.com/greek/159.htm, (1905)
[55] Lk. 4:18 and Jn. 11:1-44
[56] Ac. 4:11-12

Personal Prayer

Write a prayer of gratitude to thank Jesus for the process He went through for us. Also, pray over your personal process with God.

_____

_____

_____

_____

_____

_____

_____

_____

_____

_____

_____

_____

_____

_____

_____

_____

_____

_____

_____

_____

_____

_____

DAY
ELEVEN

Complete Surrender

Consequently, when Christ came into the world, he said, "Sacrifices and offerings you have not desired, but a body have you prepared for me. Behold, I have come to do your will, O God, as it is written of me in the scroll of the book. You have neither desired nor taken pleasure in sacrifices and offerings and burnt offerings and sin offering. And by that, will we have been sanctified through the offering of the body of Jesus Christ once for all."
—*Hebrews 10:5, 7-8, 10 (ESV)*

Christ's ultimate act of surrender for us was in the Garden of Gethsemane. Jesus knew what He would soon experience which led Him to wrestle within Himself. He was about to accomplish His Father's will. Saving us was something He desperately wanted to do; yet He still struggled with what it would take to accomplish it. If He did not follow through, He knew all of humanity would be subject to eternal separation from God. So excruciating was His experience, He needed encouragement not to give up. He asked His disciples to pray with Him for one hour, but they fell asleep.[57]

Our Savior needed prayer for His soul. He knew the prayers of His disciples would benefit Him and all of humanity. This was not a selfish request. Jesus prayed for Peter to be kept and told him so. Jesus needed prayer from His disciples to be kept as well. He requested their help to be able to finish the Father's will and bring about reconciliation between man and God. Had the disciples prayed for their Savior's strength to surrender and finish, they would have effectively prayed for the salvation of all who lived, including themselves.

---

[57] Mt. 26:36–46; Mk. 14:32–42

The disciples did not know how precious and necessary their prayers were for their beloved teacher. At a critical moment, an angel came to encourage Him and give Him strength.[58] God always sends help. When we fail to pray for our brothers and sisters, God will still send heavenly help if we ask for ourselves. Think about it. If our Savior needed prayer from His disciples and He was perfect without sin, how much more do we need to intercede for each other to be kept from falling and to live the will of our Father?

If the sacrifices of animals could cover our sin, there would be no need for Christ's surrender. Hebrews 10:5-10 tells us Jesus surrendered to the will of the Father based on what He knew was predicted of Him. This surrender is part of our sanctification process. Had He not surrendered, we would all be lost. The only way Jesus was able to surrender in this manner was by wrestling in prayer. In His wrestling, He sacrificed any desire for self-preservation. He chose to wrestle, surrender, and sacrifice because of His love for our Father and for us.

Every one of us will face personal Gethsemane experiences in our relationship with God. We will wrestle with ourselves to surrender to the Father's will as Christ did. But we will not have to do it on our own. As Christ requested His disciples to pray for Him, He is always praying for us.[59] Jesus did it for us, so He can do it through us.

---

[58] Mt. 26:36-46, Lk. 22:39-46
[59] Hb. 7:25

Reflection Questions

➤ Understanding how much our Savior needed and desired intercession from His companions, what outlook does this give you on praying for other people?

➤ What are we assured of based on Hebrews 7:25?

➤ How does this assurance encourage you?

_____

_____

_____

_____

_____

_____

_____

_____

_____

_____

_____

_____

_____

_____

_____

_____

_____

_____

_____

_____

_____

_____

_____

_____

_____

_____

_____

_____

_____

_____

_____

_____

_____

_____

_____

_____

_____

_____

_____

_____

_____

_____

Personal Prayer

Father I thank you for your Son, Jesus Christ, who prayed for me before I knew He loved me. I ask that you teach me to pray for others as He prays for me. Please place people on my heart and mind. Give me discernment through your Spirit and show me what to pray for as you lead me to pray for my brothers and sisters. Thank you for hearing and answering this prayer. In Jesus' name, Amen.

PART THREE

Christ
Our High Priest

DAY
TWELVE

Why God Established the Priesthood

"Since then, we have a great high priest who has passed through the heavens, Jesus, the Son of God. For every high priest chosen from among men is appointed to act on behalf of men in relation to God. He can deal gently with the ignorant and wayward, since he himself is beset with weakness."

—Hebrews 4:14 a, b; 5:1a, 2 (ESV)

God established the priesthood of intercession for His people so they could come to Him for forgiveness and strength and to foreshadow what Christ would soon do for them. Jesus is our High Priest and He can intercede for us better than any human. If you have gone through a particular experience, you are better equipped to minister and pray for someone who is experiencing something similar. You may or may not have known what to ask for in prayer during your experience. If you didn't, you may have sought the Father and asked Him to give you what He knew you needed. Having experienced what someone else is experiencing allows you to intercede for them because you've been through it. You've braved it. Your prayers have been answered and now you can ask the Father to give to them what He gave to you. You are able to pray from a place of experience and genuine, heartfelt intercession and even anguish based on the severity of the situation because you understand their dilemma in your soul.

That is how Christ prays for us as High Priest. The high priests of Israel were men who experienced weakness and could understand others' experiences and struggles. God's chosen priests may have experienced more dilemmas and hardships because of their roles and can empathize greatly with the people. These shared experiences may have led to more effective, heartfelt prayers from the priests and not simply routine, sacrificial prayers of obligatory kindness. They were able to stand before the Father and say, *"Lord, this is what your people are dealing with and we need all the help we can get. If we don't get help from you, we are nothing."*

The priests were held to higher standards because they represented the role Jesus would ultimately fill as High Priest; a man who understood weakness but chose not to sin. Although Jesus had weaknesses in His flesh, He had no shortcomings or mistakes and did not sin willfully. He took everything to God. If the high priests sinned willfully, they angered God: not a mistake or shortcoming, but willful sin. The high priests were to be men of standard, an example for how the Israelites should live. When Jesus came to Earth, He put on the flesh and prayed. He shared in the experience of the high priests of Israel before He fulfilled the role of the ultimate High Priest where He intercedes for us.

The priests of Israel were a foreshadowing of what Jesus would be for us: a man of standard, consecrated to God, who understood the weaknesses of the flesh, so He could cry out for others to be kept the way God kept Him. The Messiah was a human like us and overcame so we can overcome. He put on flesh to have the right to intercede for us. We can find ourselves in difficult situations due to our own sin, someone else's sin, rough circumstances, or sinful hereditary traits. But we must understand that God can use these things to bring out the priest or priestess in us. We can conquer sin by the power of Christ. We may despise life during trials and difficult moments, but someone else can benefit from our experiences. Just as Christ does for us, we can bless others through prayer and minister to them in the way they need.

Reflection Questions

➤ What makes Christ an effective intercessor as our High Priest?

➤ How can your prayers be effective for someone in a way that someone else's may not be?

➤ Why were the high priests held to a higher standard than the other people of Israel?

Personal Growth

• How does understanding the high priests' calling to a higher standard impact how you will pray about the growth of your personal relationship with the Father? How you will intercede for others?

• Based on today's reading, write a prayer that takes into account someone else's current circumstance with which you can relate.

_____

_____

_____

_____

_____

_____

_____

_____

_____

_____

DAY
THIRTEEN

Priesthood Responsibility

"For every high priest chosen from among men is appointed to act on behalf of men in relation to God, to offer gifts and sacrifices for sins. And no one takes this honor for himself, but only when called by God, just as Aaron was."

—Hebrews 5:1, 4 (ESV)

The distinguished rank of the high priest came with heavy responsibilities for Israel's relationship with God. A high priest's sins were not considered his alone; they were considered to be those of the people as well.[60] The high priest ensured his cleanliness before God because God viewed his sin as belonging to the people. As a representative of Christ, the high priest could not willfully sin. If the high priest made a mistake or unintentionally sinned, it was his responsibility to make it right with God.[61]

Two things could happen if the high priest had unforgiven sin. If he did something inadvertently and did not make it right with God, his solidarity and priestly alliance with Israel would have been obstructed. He could not be a reconciler for the people of Israel, as Christ was, because his relationship with God would be sullied. As Israel's example for holiness, if the high priest committed sin willfully, the people would follow his lead. He would not have been able to stand in the gap and intercede for the sins of the nation, having led the people into sin by his example. That would counter what Christ did for us.

Since Christ is the ultimate High Priest and we are being

---

[60] Lv. 4:3
[61] Lv. 4:1-21

restored in His image, He makes us over to live a pure life through Him and free from willful sin. A high priest's willful sin would cast a false depiction of Christ as the sinless Messiah. It would suggest that Christ would choose to sin and conform to the image of the enemy and we would follow His example, since the role of the high priest foreshadowed Christ's role as our ultimate High Priest. This is why the sins of the high priest were attributed to the people. Since Christ had no sin and the sin of the High Priest belongs to the people, no sin belongs to us as Christ-followers.

Given this, we can see the importance of the high priest's, relationship with God. The high priest bore responsibility for the nation of Israel just as Christ bears responsibility for the world. The high priest could offer sacrifices for the sins of the people, other priests, and himself. Only the high priest could officiate the sacrifices following consecration for himself or another priest.

Jesus is the only one that can cover a multitude of sins because He is the ultimate High Priest. He established a perfect connection with our Heavenly Father so we can have the same fellowship. When God looks at us, He does not see our sin; instead, He sees the righteousness of His Son.[62] Christ's right-standing with the Father is our right-standing with the Father. We are righteous because Christ is our righteousness. We are holy because Christ is our holiness. We are reconciled to the Father because Christ is our reconciliation. Christ is High Priest and made us to be a kingdom of priests. We can stand before the Father and offer sacrifices of prayer in confidence just as Jesus did.[63]

---

[62] 1 Co. 1:30 and 2 Co. 5:21
[63] Rm. 8:29 and Hb. 2:11; The high priest is always a firstborn son.

Reflection Questions

- ➤ To whom did the sin of the High Priest belong?
- ➤ Why was this important?
- ➤ Name two possible outcomes of unconfessed sin by the priest.
- ➤ How did the role of high priest affect Israel's outlook on the Messiah?
- ➤ How does the high priest having no sin reflect what Christ has done for us?
- ➤ How does the Father see us because of Christ?
- ➤ Based on today's reading, explain how we should view our relationship with God if we are part of a kingdom of priests.

Personal Prayer

Write a heartfelt prayer of gratitude for what Christ has done. Ask Him to use today's reading to shape your life.

_____

_____

_____

_____

_____

_____

_____

_____

_____

_____

_____

_____

DAY
FOURTEEN

Chosen and Appointed

"And no one takes this honor for himself, but only when called by God, just as Aaron was. So also, Christ did not exalt himself to be made a high priest, but was appointed by him who said to him, 'You are my Son, today I have begotten you.'"

—*Hebrews 5:4-5 (ESV)*

Aaron was chosen and appointed as priest as Christ was. Aaron was the first high priest for the nation of Israel, chosen by God to be an example. He was also the first born of his siblings. Whoever was chosen to be high priest had to be the first-born son in their family. This was an example of Christ being chosen from among men and being the first-born Son of God. God chose Aaron and Christ to be priests and has chosen us to be a kingdom of priests.[64] God has chosen and appointed us as priests to intercede on the behalf of others. We serve the same role as Aaron did for Israel and Christ does for us.

When we are reconciled in our relationship to God, we are not in a relationship with God only for ourselves. We are in a relationship with God for others as well. The Father calls us to minister as Christ ministered. Everything He did was for the Father and the salvation of humanity. The purpose of His relationship was for us to be saved and our relationship is meant to help others in their process. God has chosen us just as Aaron was chosen from the first-born sons and as Christ was chosen from men.

We are called to be a kingdom of priests and a holy nation to those who need us. God has chosen us to be instruments of

---

[64] Ex. 19:6 and 1 Pt. 2:9

grace and reconciliation to those in need of salvation, beginning with praying as Jesus prayed. The fellowship of reconciliation is a channel of love. We are conduits to bring others into relationships with the Father through Christ. Jesus died so anyone who accepts Him as Lord and Savior can stand before God and intercede for the souls of others. We are called to be a kingdom of priests and can bring to Christ anything that hinders our connection to the Father. We can be confident to know when God looks at us, He sees us as blameless and sinless as Jesus.[65] We can confidently bring others to God in prayer and offer sacrifices of prayer on their behalf. We know God will do the same for them as He has done for us who have been made priests because of His Son. As believers, we have all been chosen to intercede and supplicate in prayer as Christ does for us.

Since we are chosen by God like Aaron and Christ, we are appointed to pray as they did. The word for *appoint* in Hebrews 5:5 is *kathistémi*. It is a compound word with *kata* meaning *down* and *hístēmi* meaning *to stand*. The combined words mean to "set down in place; put in charge, give standing (authority, status) which enables someone to rule (exercise decisive force)."[66]

In the original language, the word *appoint* is not in Hebrews 5:5. The original language states that God spoke to His Son and told Him who He was. The use of the word *appointed*, inserted in the English version, refers to how Aaron's appointment as priest, in Hebrews 5:1, reflected Christ's appointment. When the Father chooses and appoints someone for a specific role or cause, He gives them the necessary

---

65 2 Co. 5:21

66 Gleason Archer and Gary Hill, Helps Word-Studies, https://biblehub.com/greek/2525.htm, (2011)

authority to help them perform their duties. The authority He gives comes by the power of the Holy Spirit through His Son. God will use us to offer up prayers with decisive faith and force to penetrate the heavens and set things in motion in others' and our own lives. He gives us this authority to bring about His perfect will concerning us.

Having all authority, Jesus intercedes for us and we have been given all authority to intercede for others. He has given us authority to establish things as He does through the power of prayer. Because of this, we have authority over the enemy by our connection to God in prayer. By Christ's authority, we are able to pray for others to be reconciled to The Father. When they have been reconciled, they become part of the fellowship of the kingdom of priests and learn to do for others what we have done for them.

Reflection Questions

➤ What has God chosen us to be?

➤ In your own words, explain the meaning of *kathistémi*. What does it mean for the believer in Christ?

➤ What should stem from fellowship with God?

➤ What does our intercession for others do for them?

Personal Prayer

- Write a list of names of people who God has put on your heart for intercession. What do you believe God is leading you to pray for on their behalf?
- Based on today's reading, write a prayer thanking God for what He has done for you and those on your intercessory prayer list.

_____

_____

_____

_____

_____

_____

_____

_____

_____

_____

_____

_____

_____

_____

_____

_____

_____

_____

_____

_____

_____

DAY
FIFTEEN

Our Obligation

"Because of this, he is obligated to offer sacrifice for his own sins just as he does for those of the people. And no one takes this honor for himself, but only when called by God, just as Aaron was. So also, Christ did not exalt himself to be made a high priest, but was appointed by him who said to him, 'You are my Son, today I have begotten you.'"

—Hebrews 5:3-5 (ESV)

We are called by God to be a kingdom of priests. Our calling shows we are chosen and appointed to intercede for others and we are obligated to do so. An obligation can conjure up thoughts of dread and give the sense of being required to do something but without much enthusiasm. It brings to mind how a typical teenager may respond to being asked to perform routine chores around the home. For the gospel, the meaning of *obligation* implies responsibility but does not carry the weight of an undesirous burden.

The word for *obligation* is *opheilo*. It refers to the commitment a person has to someone else because of their relationship with God. In the Bible, *opheilo* has two meanings. In the New Testament, the first is from a moral, legal, or ethical obligation; a person has to act in a certain way or do a certain thing. An example would be the high priest who must offer gifts and sacrifices because of his appointment to the position. The second is the commitment someone has when they owe a debt.[67]

Hebrews 2:17 explains that Christ became indebted to His

---

[67] Gleason Archer and Gary Hill, Helps Word-Studies, https://biblehub.com/greek/3784.htm, (2011)

Father and us. He didn't have to take on the responsibility but He chose to. Humanity became indebted to God because of sin. We owed God our lives and Christ took on the responsibility for us. He decided to be indebted to us and God. He became God incarnate to pay our debt and fulfill the debt we owed Him, because He is God. Christ made a way for us to give God our lives without paying the price of death. He became a man, lived a human life, and conquered sin so He could restore us back to our original state before sin entered our world. We were made in His image and for His glory. Jesus did not have to take on the responsibility He did for us; He did it out of love.

Obligation is birthed from desire because of love. Through love, Christ-followers can see the condition they were rescued from, the resulting freedom, and how they can be used to help save someone else from bondage. They have tasted it. They live it and walk in it. The difference between our obligation and Christ's is He was born into bondage by choice. He chose to identify with us and bring freedom because of His deep love for us. When we accept Him and become part of His kingdom of priests, He bestows love to us to give to others. Christ's love helps us identify with them and intercede for them as needed.

God allows us the choice to pray for others. While He has given us the responsibility to intercede, we don't have to do it. The responsibility of intercession may come with internal tension: tension birthed from a place of love where we want to pray for others to experience the kind of relationship we have with God. If we love as He loves, our relationship with God will lead us to intercede for others.

Can we labor in prayer for people at times? Yes. Can intercession exhaust us when we pray with fervency for others at certain times? Yes. Can it feel as if our prayers have gone unanswered because we do not see immediate results? Yes. But it must be understood that our labor in prayer will mirror how Christ labored for us while He was here. It is a labor of true love, fervent with God's desires, that we express for others.

True love wants the best for everyone. When we are called into fellowship of the priestly order, we learn to experience a heart of true love and pray for them because God has made us ministers of reconciliation. The Father has entrusted us with this particular ministry of intercession.[68]

Reflection Questions

➤ In your own words explain the meaning of *opheiló*.

➤ How did Christ *obligate* Himself to us?

➤ How does Christ's actions set an example for us?

➤ What is the most important element of our relationship with God that moves us to intercede for others?

➤ What ministry has God entrusted to us?

Personal Prayer

• Ask God to give you His love for others so you can pray for them as they need.

• Say a prayer for the people that God places on your heart today.

_____

_____

_____

_____

_____

[68] 2. Co. 5:17-20

DAY
SIXTEEN

Christ Our Gift and Sacrifice

"For every high priest chosen from among men is appointed to act on behalf of men in relation to God, to offer gifts and sacrifices for sins."

—Hebrews 5:1 (ESV)

Christ is our *gift* as well as our *sacrifice*. Hebrews 5:1 tells us that the high priest offered gifts and sacrifices for sins. Two words in the text describe the totality of what was given to us by Christ as our sacrifice. He was not only a sacrifice for us. He is also a gift we receive. In the old covenant, there were different types of sacrifices offered by the high priest that all pointed to Christ. Each of the sacrificial offerings gave a complete depiction of Christ's sacrifice.

One of the *offerings* was the *gift offering*. Scholars originally believed gift offerings were voluntary sacrifices and were typically given alone. Sometimes, however, the Israelites would offer them along with the burnt sacrifice. Gift offerings consisted of grain, frankincense, and oil.[69] The grain could either be raw and mixed with oil, mixed with oil and cooked into unleavened bread, or cooked into wafers and spread with oil. The burnt offering was either a bull, sheep, or goat and was slaughtered and offered each day for an individual's general state of sin.[70]

These two offerings reveal God's heart towards humanity. Scripture tells us that Christ is the lamb, slain from the time the world was founded, and that the Father chose us to be blameless and holy before Him in love even before then.[71]

---

[69] Lv. 2:1-16; 6:14-18; 7:9-10; 10:12-13

[70] Lv. 1:1-17

[71] Rv. 13:8 and Ep. 1:4

What does this tell us about Christ being a *gift*? The word for *gift* in Hebrews 5:1 expresses something that is freely given and has not been acquired by merit or entitlement. It reveals a brand of giving that highlights the benevolence of the giver to the recipient. We have no merit that would require Christ to give Himself for us. We did not and cannot earn our salvation. We were indebted to Him; but instead, He indebted Himself to us.

When it comes to sacrifice, we don't necessarily want to give up what we have. We do so because we understand it provides for something better to come. When a gift is given, it is understood that it is something the giver wants to do, even though it is not necessary.

The Godhead values us so much that, before the world was ever created, they were already in communication about what would happen when man chose to sin. Exchanges between the Father and Son on behalf of man pre-existed Jesus' walk on Earth. A covenant of eternal life for humanity was made by God the Father through His Son for us before creation.[72] Christ talked to the Father about helping us and lived as one of us to win us back. The Father had already planned to send Christ to win us back because of His love for us.[73] The Father chose His Son to be the Savior of the world and Christ wanted to do it. They agreed Christ would be the sacrificial gift. They didn't have to do it, but they wanted to. *"For God did not appoint us to suffer wrath, but to receive salvation through our Lord Jesus Christ."*[74]

The communication between the Father and Son is how God desires to communicate with us when we pray. He wants the thoughts and desires that are exchanged between us to be

---

[72] Ti. 1:1-2
[73] Jn. 17:24
[74] 1 Th. 5:9

on one accord. Christ's relationship with the Father has always been engaging communication, one of love and sacrifice for both of Them. The Father gave His Son as a sacrificial gift because of His love for us and to fulfill His Son's desires. Christ chose to be that sacrifice because of His love for us. Christ is our gift and sacrifice.

Reflection Questions

➤ What was the purpose of the Old Testament sacrifices?

➤ What is generally believed about the purpose of gift offerings?

➤ In your own words, explain the difference between a sacrifice and a gift.

➤ How does understanding a sacrifice and gift offering help you understand what Christ has done for you?

➤ Explain the desire of the Father and Son towards us.

➤ How does reading about the conversations between Christ and the Father regarding salvation before sin, personally impact your view of Christ's intercession for us? Does it cause you to think differently about how your conversations with God should be for others and yourself?

Personal Prayer

Based on today's reading, say a prayer of gratitude. Take time to reflect on His love today and pray for those He places on your heart.

_____

_____

_____

_____

DAY
SEVENTEEN

Christ Becoming Our High Priest

"And being made perfect, he became the source of eternal salvation to all who obey him, being designated by God a high priest after the order of Melchizedek."

—Hebrews 5:9-10 (ESV)

God's creative process is one of His most amazing attributes. We know Jesus was the creative agent of the Godhead because we are told that everything was made by Him and nothing was made without Him.[75] When God exercises His creative process, He first thinks and decides what to create. Second, He verbally expresses His thoughts and decisions. Third, what He has verbally expressed materializes. When God speaks something, there is an expectation that it will happen. Everything He speaks is nascent with possibility and outcome. His words are not sterile. Whenever He makes a decision, He speaks it and His word brings forth what He intends it to do.

The process of God's creation is expressed in the physical universe of created things and His will for the life of His Son. When God the Father decided Jesus would be a priest after the order of Melchezidek, He spoke it and Jesus went through the process to become it. Jesus is the Word Himself. Jesus had to become what was already expressed in Himself from before the beginning of time. Just as a seed houses the genetic expression of what type of plant it will become, so Christ contained the expression of humanity before He exited eternity

---

[75] Jn. 1:1-18

and entered time to fulfill it.

When we look at Hebrews 5:5-6, we see the first part of this process. The Father tells Jesus He is His begotten Son. In the following verse, God expresses His plan for His Son as High Priest. He spoke His decision for His will to be done. Just as God calls and names prophets, priests, and kings, He called His Son to His destiny.

Hebrews 5:10 gives emphasis to the second part of the process where God speaks a word over the life of His Son. The word used to define this part of His process is *designated*. The translated meaning is "to address, call by name, to give a name to publicly." He calls Him by name according to His plan. The Father pronounced Jesus as His Son and High Priest. He also calls us to become His sons and daughters and a kingdom of priests.[76] The Father has publicly declared His desired will for us. It has been given to us in His Son Jesus Christ and in His word.

The way Jesus received the word from His Father regarding His will is the same way we are to receive it. He received it through connection and communication with the Father. Jesus communicated continually with His Father, even before the beginning of the world. This is how the Father pronounced Jesus as His begotten Son and a priest after the order of Melchezidek. They were in communication before the world and the entrance of sin. In the same way, we must communicate with God for Him to proclaim our identity and for us to understand His will. We are to depend on every word from the Father the way Jesus did. God expects us to receive His word over our life the way Christ did. The only way we can receive from God is to remain connected to the Father in

---

[76] Rv. 1:6 and 2 Co. 6:18

prayer and surrender.

The third part of the process is Jesus' transformation into what His Father called Him to be. He walked according to the word spoken over His life. In Hebrews 6:20, God says of Jesus, *"Having become a priest forever after the order of Melchizedek."* He could only *become* this through the process of what He endured while on Earth. We must do the same.

When God calls us by name, He expects us to step into the relationship with Him and allow Him to form us according to His will. We must step into the plan God has for us as His sons and daughters and become part of His kingdom of priests. We must also be willing to undergo transformation into the image of Christ and fulfill His purpose for creating us. We are called to a higher order. We are called to be intercessors. We are called as kings and priests. We are called to God Himself.

The enemy has done an excellent job of creating fear and disinterest within us about our true identity. We are sons and daughters of the Most High. God has created us for His glory.[77] Jesus expresses His will for us in a prayer of intercession in John 17:22: "The glory that you have given me, I have given to them that they may be one even as we are one."

We are created beings; Jesus thought of us and decided to make us. We are also created beings because of His will for our lives. The plan of salvation is harmonious with the plan of creation. God's salvation project was prearranged as a part of our restoration process to become a new creation through the life of Christ. This plan was thought up, spoken, and lived out through Christ. He became what we are, so we can become what He is. We are children of God and royal priests. We are God restored in man, reconciled to Him, and are in a right-

---

[77] Is. 43:7

relationship with the Father through Jesus because of the process He went through for us.

Reflection Questions

➢ Briefly describe how God expresses His will for us and how we are to receive it.

➢ Based on today's reading, what is the ploy of the enemy?

➢ What has God made through His Son, based on today's reading?

Personal Prayer

If you don't know Jesus Christ as your personal Savior, write a prayer inviting Him to be. Pray for yourself to know His will and for restoration in your life.

_____

_____

_____

_____

_____

_____

_____

_____

_____

_____

_____

_____

_____

_____

DAY
EIGHTEEN

Forever After the Order of Melchezidek

"And he says in another place, You are a priest forever, after the order of Melchizedek. And being made perfect, he became the source of eternal salvation to all who obey him. We have this as a sure and steadfast anchor of the soul, a hope that enters into the inner place behind the curtain, where Jesus has gone as a forerunner on our behalf, having become a high priest forever after the order of Melchizedek."

—Hebrews 5:6, 9-10; 6:19-20 (ESV)

Our Father pronounced Jesus as the eternal High Priest after the order of Melchezidek after Christ ascended to heaven to begin His priestly ministry. David first prophetically spoke of it in Psalm 110:4 and the author of Hebrews quotes David. The question becomes, "Who is Melchezidek, and what does this have to do with us?" Melchezidek was a priest and the king of Salem. His story is found in Genesis 14:18-20. He was the high priest that Abraham returned a tithe to after rescuing his nephew, Lot, from Mesopotamian kings.[78]

His name means *king of righteousness* and he is considered a *king of peace* because *Salem* means *peace*. Melchezidek is the only priest in the Bible that was a king as Christ is. His office existed before God established the Levitical order, so it rightly represents the office of Christ as King and Priest. Melchezidek represents the eternal priesthood established before the Levites that continues on into eternity. Melchezidek has neither a recorded genealogy nor a recorded death, making him symbolic

---

[78] Gn. 14

of the high priesthood of Christ.

Christ's office also exists outside of the Levitical order and lasts forever from eternity. There is no beginning and no end. His office is better than that of Melchezidek because His sacrifice was once and for all, unlike animals that were sacrificed repeatedly. The animal's blood could not perfect us. Only the blood of Christ, the one who is our sacrificial gift and High Priest, could. He was slain once from the foundation of the world. If Christ's blood was not good enough to destroy sin, He would have had to die repeatedly. His sacrifice perfected us once and for all.[79] In God's eyes, it was already done. Christ is the King of righteousness that has brought us peace with the Father.

When we look at Hebrews 5:6, the Father says, *"You are a priest forever after the order of Melchezidek."* Hebrews 6:20 says, *"Jesus has gone as a forerunner on our behalf, having become a high priest forever after the order of Melchizedek."* How can Jesus become something that has no beginning or end? The answer is in the tense and definition of the Greek word for the phrase *having become*. We learned earlier the meaning of *become* in the original language: *ginomai* meaning "to emerge, become, transitioning from one point, realm or condition to another; changing in state or place." *Gínomai* is used to describe God's actions as emerging from eternity and becoming by showing themselves in physical space and time.[80]

The tense for *gínomai* in the verse is called *aorist*. It is described as "a simple occurrence or summary occurrence, without regard for the amount of time taken to accomplish the action. It can be simply viewed as a single, collective whole or

---

79 Hb. 9:23-10:18
80 Gleason Archer and Gary Hill, Helps Word-Studies, https://biblehub.com/greek/1096.htm, (2011)

a point-in-time action (past, present or future), although it may actually take place over a period of time."[81]

How does it apply to Christ as Melchezidek? The *aorist* tense defines and describes the transition of Christ as our Savior as emerging from eternity and placing Himself in time here on Earth. He came to overcome sin, become our High Priest, and exit time to return to eternity on our behalf and intercede for us so we can live forever. Even though Christ became a priest after the order of Melchezidek, His atoning work is viewed as an action for all time at once. It is eternal. It is seen in the *aorist* tense of the verb, showing how it has been covered since before we existed. Jesus, being eternal, placed Himself within the confines of time to become a priest by overcoming sin. He emerged as the anointed Messiah incarnate and took on the role of priest after His victory, *"having become,"* although it had been established since eternity. Sin has been covered since eternity and the foundation of the world.

What does that mean for us? Just as Jesus took on another role after His death, so do we when we die to our sinful nature in Him. He put on the order of priest and king after He rose from the dead. It is the same with us. When our carnal man dies, we become part of Christ in His kingdom. We take on the role of priest and king in the order of Christ as He did after Melchizedek. Jesus is eternal and those who are in Him will have eternal life. We intercede as He intercedes, and we will reign as He reigns. Christ has gone as forerunner on our behalf. He first became what we become in Him. When we become a part of His kingdom, His image and life are restored in us.[82] We become what He is—God, restored in man, with all

---

[81] Corey Keating, NTGreek.org Blog, Corey Keating, http://www.ntgreek.org/learn_nt_greek/verbs1.htm, (accessed 3/3/18)
[82] Ga. 3:27

authority over the power of the enemy.[83] He is the reigning King and has made us to reign with Him. [84] We are restored in Him in the same order of Melchezidek in communion with our Heavenly Father. We are kings and priests, a royal priesthood destined for eternity.[85]

Reflection Questions

➢ Who was Melchezidek and how did his priesthood reflect Christ?

➢ Briefly explain what *gínomai* means.

➢ Why is Christ's sacrifice the ultimate sacrifice?

➢ What has Christ's priesthood done for us? Name some of the attributes of our new standing in Christ based on today's reading.

Personal Prayer

• Write a heartfelt prayer of gratitude for what Christ has done for us and pray it out aloud.

• Claim a promise for each person that God puts on your heart to pray for today. Pray out loud and proclaim the promise over their lives to build your faith in God's promises and the authority He has given to you. It may feel funny at first but the more you do it, the more you'll get used to it.

_____

_____

_____

_____

_____

[83] Lk. 9:1, 10:19
[84] 2 Tm. 2:12
[85] Rv. 5:10; 6:1; 1 Pt 2:9

DAY
NINTEEN

The Godhead's Main Concern

"The former priests were many in number, because they were prevented by death from continuing in office, but he holds his priesthood permanently, because he continues forever. Consequently, he is able to save to the uttermost, those who draw near to God through him, since he always lives to make intercession for them."

—Hebrews 7:23-25 (ESV)

The life of Christ has always been one of communing with the Father. What is amazing about the Godhead's communion is Their particular interest in saving humanity. They laid the blueprint for the plan of salvation before the world was made and were in deep discussion about how things would play out. The love of God is so fathomless for us that they didn't wait until sin happened to devise a plan in our interest. It wasn't a *just in case this happens* plan. The plan of salvation was a plan the Godhead knew would be needed and arranged for. Humanity is so dear and important to the Godhead that they wrote an active role for us to play in our own rescue plan.

Typically, when a superhero saves a person, the one being saved has no part in the process. The hero doesn't share their glory, nor do they offer to teach the person how to fight as they do. The hero simply receives their commendation and moves on to the next rescue. The rescued person usually has one encounter with their hero never to see or hear from them again. If there is any kind of intimate exchange, it tends to be a once-in-a-lifetime thing.

Jesus, our hero, is different. He saves us, shares His glory with us, and teaches us how to fight like Him. He gave humanity an active role in saving their fellow brothers and sisters. God established the Levitical priesthood to reflect the priesthood of Christ and teach His children how to intercede on others' behalf. He taught humanity how to fight by prayer. Even with the Levitical system in place, the sacrifices given, and prayers from the priests, it wasn't enough. Hebrews 7:25 tells us that Christ lives to intercede on our behalf. The Greek word for *always* is *pantote* and it means "at all times, ever."

The Godhead's primary concern is helping humanity. Yes, they rule, reign, and create marvelous works. But the current focus of their existence is to redeem all lost souls. How great God's love is for us! For that reason, Christ is continuously praying for each one of us. He is before His Father asking for what we need. He pleads for the salvation of every person's soul. No matter how terrible of a life they have lived or how worthless that person may think they are, Christ does not see them that way. He has bought us with a price.[86] He longs for us to call on Him for help in every situation and circumstance. It is His desire and pleasure to save us and keep us from giving into temptation. Jude 1:24 says, *"Now to him who is able to keep you from stumbling and to present you blameless before the presence of his glory with great joy."* When we let Christ keep us and present us blameless to the Father, He is able to present us without the effect of sin in us. He can present us without any change in us as a result or consequence of sin we may have committed. For this to happen, we must take on His nature and allow Him to work through us. He resisted and overcame sin, so there is no effect of sin in Him. When He lives in us, He removes all sin and its effects. When He presents us to the Father, He sees the

---

[86] 1 Co. 7:23

righteousness of Jesus, not our own.

Christ is able to save anyone from any form of sin, no matter how terrible, and give them strength to overcome any weakness. Christ lived by the power of the Holy Spirit during His earthly walk. He lives in us by the Spirit, helping us in all our weaknesses. The groans Christ gave as He prayed in the Spirit for deliverance from temptation are the same groans the Holy Spirit intercedes with for us when we pray.[87] The Holy Spirit that helped Jesus pray is the same Holy Spirit that prays through us. Christ lives to intercede for us, so we can live to intercede to Him.

Reflection Questions

> Based on today's reading, how important are we to God?
> What is the primary focus of the Godhead?
> How does knowing this make you feel?
> What does Christ long for us to do and what does it do for Him?
> What is promised to us in prayer according to Romans 8: 26-27?

Personal Prayer

Write a prayer of gratitude for what God has made available to us and ask Him to keep you.

_____

_____

_____

_____

[87] Rm. 8:26-27

PART FOUR

Christ
Our Deliverance and Victory

Our Deliverance Through Christ

"Let us run with endurance the race that is set before us, looking to Jesus, the founder and perfecter of our faith, who for the joy that was set before him endured the cross, despising the shame, and is seated at the right hand of the throne of God. In your struggle against sin you have not yet resisted to the point of shedding your blood."

—Hebrews 12:1b-2, 4 (ESV)

As we are perfected like Jesus, we go through a process of deliverance from our sinful tendencies. The race we run is the walk of Christ.[88] When He felt tempted or wanted to give up, He did not hesitate to fall to His knees in prayer. Every bit of surrender He went through led to Him being our Deliverer. We can only have victory by first experiencing deliverance through Jesus Christ.

Colossians 1:12-13 says that the Father has qualified us for His inheritance and delivered us from darkness into the kingdom of His Son. The word *deliverance*, in this verse, means to "draw to oneself, to rescue, to snatch up for oneself; to draw or rescue a person to and for the deliverer." The ending of the Lord's Prayer in Matthew 6:13 can mean, *"Deliver me to yourself and for yourself."* That is, *"Lord, deliver me out of my personal pain, struggle and bring me to you for you.* [89] This was Christ's deliverance. His deliverance from the snares of the enemy was not

---

[88] Hb. 12:1-2

[89] Mt. 6:13; The word used for evil is ponéros which describes the toilsome pain of labor associated with evil. See Gleason Archer and Gary Hill, Helps Word-Studies, https://biblehub.com/greek/4190.htm, (2011).

inconsequential. He was not set free from our weaknesses to do things of His own accord. Deliverance for Jesus was about reconciling us to the Father to do His will.

People often want freedom from the stronghold of sin keeping them bound, but they don't necessarily want the responsibility that comes with that freedom. They may not be troubled by the sin itself, but they do not want its consequences. True deliverance requires us to hate the sin the same way we hate the consequences of it. Jesus hated sin; therefore, He automatically hated the consequences. His hatred for sin caused Him to suffer the effect of eternal consequences on our behalf. Jesus chose to suffer emotional and physical trauma and death rather than give in or give up.

Hebrews 12:4 says we have not *"yet"* resisted sin to the point where we shed blood. The word *"yet"* is an indication that we can resist, as Christ did, with His help. We must hate sin the way Christ does and have the faith that He will help us not to cherish it. If we allow Him to work in us, we will want to resist all sin.

Christ's resistance of sin to the point of bloodshed is two-fold. In Luke's account of Jesus praying in Gethsemane, he uses a medical term to describe Jesus' sweat turning into blood.[90] His internal battle to surrender and not give in to the temptation of giving up was so great, He shed blood: a precursor to what would take place on Calvary. If there was ever a time Jesus did not have joy, it was then. He endured the

---

[90] Lk. 22:44; Hematidrosis, or hematohidrosis, is very rare medical condition that causes you to ooze or sweat blood from your skin when you're not cut or injured. See Jaliman MD, Debra. "What is Hematidrosis." WebMD. February 15, 2018. Hematidrosis is a word of Greek origin formed from two words; haima/haimatos meaning blood and "hidrós" meaning sweat. See James Strong, "Strong's Concordance", https://biblehub.com/greek/129.htm, (1905) and James Strong, "Strong's Concordance", https://biblehub.com/greek/2402.htm (1905).

process of perfecting our deliverance because of the joy the Father promised would be waiting for Him when He finished His course.[91]

While in the garden, all Christ could see was the gripping eternal state of death for those He was sacrificing His life for. He experienced the agony of hell's separation. He was inflicted with doubts from the enemy that told Him He would not succeed. He also wrestled with the doubt that if He did go through with His sacrifice, He might not come out of the grave. It was difficult for Him to see His way out of those circumstances. He had to faithfully hold on to the word of His Father that He would be delivered from death's grip.[92] He felt the pangs of death in His soul for every soul that would and would not choose to accept His sacrifice. Even to our Savior, who is life Himself, eternal death looked so grim, He fought to resist the fearful lie that He would lose Himself and all of humanity to it.

This was the only way deliverance for humanity could come. He resisted sin by drawing close to the Father and becoming humanity's deliverance from sin and death. When we are drawn to the Father, it is by the *Way*, who is Jesus Christ. He lived as He taught us: to pray and continuously seek the Father for strength and deliverance from temptation. No one can get to the Father unless it is by Christ. He is our *way* of escape from sin.[93] Christ is now seated next to the Father, in the Most Holy Place, interceding for each of us. He prays for our deliverance so we may overcome as He did. We may still wrestle with some of our sinful tendencies, but we are part of His royal kingdom of priests and kings because He covers us

---

[91] Hb. 12:2
[92] Ps. 16:10
[93] Jn. 14:6, 1 Co. 10:13

and will complete the work He began in us.[94] As He prays to the Father for the work He began in us to be perfected, so are we to pray for the work He began in our brothers and sisters to be perfected.

Reflection Questions

> ➤ How do we experience victory?
> ➤ What was the purpose of Christ's deliverance?
> ➤ What has to happen for us to experience true victory?
> ➤ How does what happened in Gethsemane help you have more appreciation for Jesus?

Personal Prayer

Write a prayer for yourself and others, who God places on your heart, about deliverance in the areas where it is needed.

_____

_____

_____

_____

_____

_____

_____

_____

_____

_____

_____

_____

_____

_____

_____

[94] Rv. 1:6; Pp. 1:6

DAY
TWENTY
ONE

Christ Our Victory

"Therefore, brothers, since we have confidence to enter the holy places by the blood of Jesus, by the new and living way that he opened for us through the curtain, that is, through his flesh, and since we have a great priest over the house of God, let us draw near with a true heart in full assurance of faith, with our hearts sprinkled clean from an evil conscience and our bodies washed with pure water. Let us hold fast the confession of our hope without wavering, for he who promised is faithful. And let us consider how to stir up one another to love and good works."

—Hebrews 10:19-24 (ESV)

Jesus is not only our deliverance, He is our victory. Because He overcame sin and conquered death, He is able to give us His victory as our own. When we pray, we can come to the Father in confidence knowing that He accepts us because of His Son's sacrifice. The access we have is because of His blood that was shed. Without Christ's sacrifice, we would not be able to approach the Father.

Hebrews 10:20 says Jesus is the *"new and living way"* and He opened the curtain for us to the Most Holy Place. Every word in the phrase *"new living way"* explains who Christ is and what He has done for us. The Greek word for *new* in this verse is *prosphatos,* meaning "freshly slain or generally new."[95] The word for *living* is *zao,* meaning to "live, experience God's gift of life." The word for *way* is *hodos,* meaning "way or path."[96]

---

[95] James Strong, Strong's Concordance, https://biblehub.com/greek/4372.htm, (1905)
[96] James Strong, Strong's Concordance, https://biblehub.com/greek/2198.htm, (1905) and James Strong, Strong's Concordance, https://biblehub.com/greek/3598.htm, (1905)

Christ was slain to bring fulfillment to the new covenant. The old covenant was made with the blood of animals that could not save us, but Christ's blood is what gives us life.[97] Christ is our gift of life. There is no life outside of Him. Any animal that was sacrificed could not save us and remained dead: a symbol of Christ's death. He died and resurrected with victory over death.[98] He is living and reigns next to the Father.[99] Christ is our *way*. He tells us He is the *way*, the truth, and the life to the Father in Heaven.[100] He is the *way* we are to live. He is our *way* of escape from temptation. He is our *way* of deliverance. He is our *way* out of the grave. He is our *way* to the throne of grace and He is our *way* into the kingdom.

There is no other way to the Father. Jesus' flesh being pierced and torn during the crucifixion is symbolic of the veil to the Most Holy Place being torn in half for our access. We cannot get to the Father without Christ. He says, *"All things have been handed over to me by my Father, and no one knows who the Son is except the Father, or who the Father is except the Son and anyone to whom the Son chooses to reveal him."*[101] The ancient Jews allowed themselves to be hindered from believing He was sent to them because of His humanity, but that is how He had to reveal Himself. The flesh is what has blocked us from Him, and the flesh is what needed to be torn for us to reconcile with the Father. When His flesh was crucified, God in man triumphed. The curtain was torn, allowing us access to God the Father.

As Christ is our *way*, He is also our example of what we are to become: a *living sacrifice*. We are to live newly sacrificed, as Jesus has for us. We are to crucify our flesh and die daily so

---

[97] Hb. 8:7-8
[98] Rev. 1:18
[99] Rm. 8:34
[100] Jn. 14:6
[101] Lk. 10:22

Christ can live in us.[102] He has cleansed our consciences and washed us, so we will believe all He has done for us because of His faithfulness. If we do not, our flesh will hinder us from coming into a loving relationship with the Father in spite of the access He has given us to Himself. Jesus said when we look at Him, we see the Father because they are One.[103] When others see us, they should see Christ because we are to be one with Him as He is one with the Father.[104] We are to be an example of the *Way* to the Father. We are not the *Way*, but an example of Him. Our lives should help lead people to Jesus as He led us back to the Father. He put on our flesh and crucified it so we can put on His glory.

God has called us to be living sacrifices as Christ was. Our prayer life is part of sacrificial living. When we intercede for our brothers and sisters as Christ continuously prays for us, it helps to restore us to the image of God. The Father and Christ have made the salvation of humanity Their primary concern and have called us to be a kingdom of intercessors. We must mirror Their focus and make the salvation and victory of others our focus. We should be concerned with the eternal state of every soul God has us to minister to and impact. We cannot save them, only Christ can. But we are to love them as He does and serve them in accordance with God's leading. Christ's prayers for Himself were not selfish. When He prayed for Himself, it was for His relationship with the Father in order to fulfill His mission for our salvation. As intercessors, we are to pray the same way. Being an intercessor doesn't mean we don't ever pray for ourselves. It simply means God has entrusted us with a gift to bring people to the throne of grace in a way they

---

[102] Ga. 5:24, 1 Co. 15:31
[103] Jn. 14:9
[104] 1 Co. 6:17

may not be able to do for themselves. As we grow in Christ, understand Him more, and become more like Him, our prayers will reflect His. We will become more concerned about the lives of others and less concerned about ourselves. Nothing for the kingdom of God can be done without prayer. For good works to be stirred up among God's people, we must pray for one another. This is how we are to live as a kingdom of praying priests and kings.

Paul tells us that because Jesus is who He is, has done what He has done, and is seated where He is seated, we are with Him. *"By grace you have been saved and raised us up with him and seated us with him in the heavenly places in Christ Jesus."* [105] Only by the grace of God and our faith can we grab hold of the reality that we are seated in Heavenly places with Jesus. We have the victory in Jesus! He has overcome and conquered everything for us.[106]

---

[105] Ep. 2:5b-6a
[106] Jn 16:33

Reflection Questions

➢ What happened when Christ died and what is the significance of it?

➢ What are we to do daily?

➢ What kind of example are we to set to others?

➢ What should be our primary concern in this life?

➢ What will happen as we grow in relationship with Christ?

➢ What can be done for God without prayer?

➢ What is our position because of Christ?

➢ What do we have because of Jesus?

Personal Prayer

Write a prayer of thanksgiving to God and include details about the victory in your life and victory in the lives of people God has placed on your heart.

_____

_____

_____

_____

_____

_____

_____

_____

_____

_____

_____

_____

"Now to him who is able to keep you from stumbling and to present you blameless before the presence of his glory with great joy, to the only God, our Savior, through Jesus Christ our Lord, be glory, majesty, dominion, and authority, before all time and now and forever. Amen!"

Special Acknowledgments

To God: Thank you for blessing me with a gift to write and for using me to write *Priesthood Prayer*. I am grateful to be used to convey Christ's experience in identifying with us so we may know we have a Savior that truly understands our struggles.

To Wale Adepoju: Thank you for asking me to write this devotional and for all of your encouragement and prayers.

To those who specifically prayed for the writing of this devotional: Evelyna Laurie, Del Valle, Tiffany Ellis-McCourty, Carlton Green, Lisa Porter, Sara Osi, Tiffany Wilson, Krystal Kenner-Delisser, Patrice Delisser, Amanda Hawley, Dorian Gonzalez, Thessicar Antoine-Reid, Crystal S. Lewis, Marci Mayberry, Melissa Webster, Andrea Anderson, Erica Keith, Lise Calixte, Rennae Ralph, Susan T. James, Carla Ellis, Aletheia Winborn, Dr. Timothy Golden, Emmanuel St. Cloud, April Ingram, Bettye Taliaferro, Vincent Kennedy, Jason McCourty, Melissa Weathers, Geraldine Weathers and the rest of my First Coatesville SDA Church family, my Germantown SDA Church family and all others that have prayed for this project.

To those who donated money towards Priesthood Prayer: Rebecca Cowans, Toni Hall, Erica Keith, Carla Ellis, Jeremi Jones, Diana Kline, Kenneth Green II, Katherine Hughes, Tina Brody, Carlton Green, Crystal Lewis, Alisa Williams, Byronette Watson. Thank you all for your financial support.

To the Mynd Matters Publishing Team: Thank you so much for your excellent services. It was such a blessing and pleasure for my first book to be published by you. God bless you all and may God continue to smile on you and prosper you.